KV-191-371

Contents

Preface

Although I researched this book for several years prior, the bulk of it was written during the first 6 months of 2001. My observations about TV's coverage of natural disasters that took place in the early and mid-1990s was still pertinent in early 2001, and, I believe, that remains the case. However, the infamous events of September 11, 2001, forced me to quickly reassess what I had written about TV and disaster. My initial fear was that the events of that date in particular would redefine TV coverage of disaster generally, and that natural disaster coverage would seem completely off the mark, if not somehow unimportant in comparison, from that day forward. But after closely watching TV news coverage of the terrorist attacks in New York City and Washington, DC, I realized that much of what I had to say about TV natural disaster coverage applied to other kinds of disasters coverage as well. Obviously the events of September 11, 2001—captured live, instantly, and almost continuously on TV—were not natural disasters. Yet I found as I watched that what I had to say about TV treatment of natural disaster applied in many ways to TV treatment of the horror and ensuing chaos of the September events that occurred that day and unfolded for a long while thereafter.

Despite the obvious differences between floods in the rural U.S. midwest and attacks on two major urban structures in the eastern United States, I noted significant similarities in the way they were recreated on TV. In the flood, as in the terrorist attacks, TV took an unprecedented and unpredicted event and broadcast it in a rather predictable way. The TV camera focused on, framed, and revisited over and over again the most dramatic images of the event. Visual images chosen during the first live and unfolding coverage, and in news packages in the days that followed, were edited to underscore the chaos and horror. Along with signature visuals, music, graphics and a host of titles created specifically by the networks for this event served as reminders and rallying signifiers of the horror. They also pointed us in a particular direction as they set the agenda of our national discourse concerning the terrorist attacks and preparing us for the proper national response.

Visual images on TV news reinforced to a large degree the wartime atmosphere that quickly took over the nation. Two specific visual images used over and over during TV news coverage of the September 11th attacks were footage of the Twin Towers of the World Trade Center being hit, burning, and/or collapsing, and the American flag. The flag, of course, has always been symbolic of the nation. In terrorist attack TV coverage, it became a symbol of patriotic zeal and was used as a badge of solidarity on the news set in a number of different graphic incarnations. Because of the way the Twin Tower footage was edited into newscasts in many different contexts, it became a metaphor for American national identity as well as a metaphor for American privilege and loss. It was also, of course, a constant reminder of the attack and, because of its jarring visual impact, a justification for retaliation. Such images, like most images on TV news, only offer us the present. Although, to its credit, many TV newscasts did try to put the events of that day into historical context in an effort to explain how such a thing could have happened, it is important to note that, on TV, it is about the visuals, not the words.

Television is a visual electronic medium. Its emphasis is on right now. During disaster coverage of any sort, it is preoccupied with the beautiful and the horrid. Thanks to sophisticated digital technology, TV news personnel can create amazing visuals and edited sequences, highlighting the drama that is essential to news. Television news visuals are becoming more dense, and more quickly paced, and graphics are becoming more sophisticated. Words are secondary to visuals. The conversation about the disaster on TV is about the pictures. In terrorist coverage, words explaining the historical context are submerged beneath the daily onslaught of video footage of Ground Zero, the face of Osama bin Laden, and the maps of Afghanistan. Television shows us what is happening right now and where it is happening.

In this book, I analyze natural disaster TV news, and put particular emphasis on the connection between nature and place, or geographic identity. I argue that TV, because of the way it represents disaster events, in fact re-creates them in a completely different way for the screen. In the process, and because of the inherent characteristics of the medium, TV has changed the way we think about nature and place. The same can be said of other kinds of disaster coverage, including the disaster created for the small screen on and following September 11, 2001. The point is that TV is a powerful medium and not just because it provides us with up-to-the-minute coverage of events taking place both near us and far away.

Television is still currently the dominant tool of our cultural conversation, as Postman (1985) argued. It is powerful because it can create visually something entirely different from what occurs off screen. Most people still choose the visual re-creation on the TV screen as their source for understanding what has happened and is happening. Therefore, TV news sets the agenda for discussions and actions following events that have important environmental and political impact. For this reason, it is urgent that we understand the routines of TV journalism—specifically how and why TV news visuals are put together, particularly in a situation that makes for dramatic pictures. Clearly, there is much more to understand about TV news and disaster. Clearly, my work has just begun.

Acknowledgments

This book has been in the making for several years. And, like any major undertaking, was made possible because of the patience, expertise, and interest of many people, not just the author. Therefore I would like to acknowledge the debt I owe to all those who provided just what I needed, at just the right time, while I conducted research, assembled information, and wrote the manuscript. My apologies to anyone I may have mistakenly omitted from this list.

First I must thank the PSC-CUNY Research Foundation for providing much-needed funds that allowed me to assemble network news videotape and to travel in the midwest, collecting local news information and interviews. This book is a direct result of that financial support.

A number of people gave me access to local television newsrooms and news footage. These include the news stations and staff of KCCI, KMOV, KSDK, and WHBF. Special thanks to Pete Barrett, Lisa Molina, Bob Garger, Erika Herrmann, Marc McLaughlin, and Scott Faber.

For taking the time to talk at great length with me about their newsgathering and news generating experiences, I thank the following network correspondents and other network news personnel: David Abbate, Tom Foreman, John Gibson, Paul Hammons, Erin Hayes, Kenley Jones, Vickie Mabrey, and Scott Pelle. And to Mike Brue and Terry Dullum at WDAZ.

Thanks also to Frances Ford who very generously took the time to explain to me about her performance and what it was like to be in Grand Forks, North Dakota after the flood.

My thanks to graduate students Allon Hanania and Hiroshi Sato who helped me tremendously by viewing and coding news footage and providing unique cultural insight.

The Department of Television and Radio at Brooklyn College was very supportive of this research effort, and I must thank especially Hal Himmelstein and Kathy Napoli who both helped in their own specific ways to make this manuscript come together.

While writing in Minnesota I was given access to, and used extensively, library facilities at the University of Minnesota, Macalester College and St. Thomas University.

For technical expertise, guidance, and great generosity I owe an enormous debt to Israela Loeb and John Gaspard; for the kind of support one needs during that all-consuming task of writing I thank David Brown and Jeanette Turner; and for taking such an interest and helping to shepherd this manuscript to completion, a very big thanks to Lance Strate at Fordham University, and Barbara Bernstein and Joni Choi at Hampton Press.

The biggest thanks go to family members who provided support of every kind, especially as I prepared the manuscript. The kindness and generosity of these people are unparalleled in my universe and most likely all others. Special thanks to my parents, Henry and Ruth Fry, to Neal and Donna Nickerson and all of the midwest Nickerson clan, to Jim and Rachel Cunningham for unbelievable patience and hospitality, and to Sarah Schendel for being the solid rock that she is.

Finally, there is no way to express in print what I owe to the three Nickersons who live with me, offer unconditional love and praise, and remind me in many ways who I am and how important my work is. Thanks to Liv who was born right in the middle of all this, to Noah who has come to understand bit by bit what this is, and to Jay, my very best, most enthusiastic, most patient of all supporters who has always known what this is.

While I acknowledge the great help provided by all those listed, I alone take full responsibility for everything that is here written.

Katherine Fry
Brooklyn, New York
April 2003

Introduction

. . . it has been a world class fight. The engineers constructed tidy bound-
aries and are furiously protecting them. From the front line the effort has
been heroic, but look at it from up here and it looks pretty insignificant.
Many have accepted that in this fight of the century, the decision goes to
the river.

It's frustrating to a society that conquered the moon and space to think that
a long-held claim to river land has been so soundly rejected by nature so
easily. But that is in a river's nature.

—Erin Hayes, "ABC Evening News," July 29, 1993

In 1993, after unusually heavy spring and summer rainfalls and quickly
melting snow, the upper Mississippi River and its tributaries flooded
their banks in many places to historically unprecedented heights. Nine
midwestern states were affected by flooding on 6.5 million acres of land
because of 250% normal summer rainfall between June and August of
that year. Heavy flooding displaced homes, businesses, and farms
throughout the region. The cost of the flood in the midwest region as a
whole was approximately $18 billion in damages. In all, 525 counties in

1

the nine midwestern states were declared natural disaster areas because of the 1993 flood (Anderson & Platt, 1999). As early as March 1993, the three major broadcast networks—ABC, CBS, and NBC—began periodically reporting on this escalating flood. By late June and until at least September, nearly every night the three networks broadcast flood news mostly from the Mississippi River and its tributaries in three states: Iowa, Illinois, and Missouri. Flood news focused on areas in those three states sustaining the greatest damage to farms, homes, and businesses on the flood plain, and to towns built along riverbanks.

July 22, 1993, is an example of a typical day of network reporting during the height of the flood. On that day, ABC, CBS, and NBC all devoted 4 to 5 minutes of air time to the latest damages across the region. Early in the day, a stressed levee protecting Kaskaskia Island, Illinois had finally burst. Quickly homes and entire farms were submerged. The three networks were there, framing and transmitting pictures of the scene using extreme long shots from cameras situated in helicopters hovering high above the flooding Island and on the ground where the waters had not yet encroached. The air shots dramatically captured the breadth of the disaster while on the ground close shots of evacuated residents captured the emotional dimensions of their loss. One farmer interviewee resigned himself to his loss as he lamented in close shot, "Old Man River won this time." The networks also reported that, on that same day, the residents of Des Moines, Iowa were finally able to use water from the municipal water supply, which had been shut off for over a week because the reservoir had flooded with contaminated river water. Interviewees on camera demonstrated their delight at once again being able to take a shower and flush the toilet. ABC's Peter Jennings, on location in downtown Des Moines, recounted for viewers that a columnist for the *Des Moines Register* had surmised in that day's paper that perhaps the flood was God's reply to riverboat gambling, which had not long before been legalized. The networks that day also emphasized the economic consequences to the region and the nation. CBS reported that flooding on the Mississippi River, an important economic waterway for the nation, was causing a huge loss for shippers of food, auto parts, coal, and steel to the rest of the nation and beyond.

On that day, and most every day of flood coverage, all three networks told the flood story via a variety of images and words and from a number of different perspectives. The story was shaped by the medium and broadcast over the network infrastructure to the entire nation. Network news personnel relied on a particular understanding of the geographic area and its people as well as the routine formulations of TV news to guide the footage they shot and edited, and to determine how they would piece together what became a distinct narrative of midwest flooding, midwest flood victims, and attempts to control the continuing chaos. Television news was one such attempt.

In 1997, TV had another midwest flood story to tell. In April of that year, another major flood hit the midwest. This time it was the Red River and its tributaries flooding way beyond capacity. In the United States, the flood affected most profoundly Minnesota and North Dakota. The winter of 1996 to 1997 was one blizzard after another in the northern portion of the midwest. Months of record amounts of snowfall culminated in a spring thaw the likes of which the Red River was unable to confine along its normal path. The river spilled over onto farms and towns along its northerly route into Canada. The flooding and overall brutal weather conditions that year resulted in the loss of hundreds of thousands of acres of farmland, the death of 100,000 cattle, and the temporary displacement of the entire city of Grand Forks, North Dakota (Reuter, 1998). Once again the three major broadcast networks traveled to the midwest to cover a flood. This one affected a smaller area, and didn't unfold over as long a time period as the 1993 flood, but national and local television reported that flood in a similar way.

NATURAL DISASTERS ON TV NEWS

It is common practice in TV to broadcast news of natural disaster, thereby informing those in the immediately affected areas and far beyond. It is also common knowledge to audience members that TV can and will offer them almost instant dramatic images of natural disaster from around the world. In fact, it is becoming more and more common. Federal funding for natural disasters greatly increased during the 1990s. The United Nations declared the 1990s as the International Decade for Natural Disaster Reduction (Platt, 1999). A major reason for increased funding for and attention to natural disaster, some argue, is because of an increase in reporting and documenting natural disaster loss, particularly on TV. It has been called the *CNN syndrome* (Platt, 1999). Easily we take for granted the amount—in detail, sheer volume, and intensity—of TV news about earthquakes, floods, forest fires, hurricanes and other such "acts of God" from all over the world. Yet despite the breadth of coverage, we seldom reflect on the quality or the implications of natural disaster news on TV. What do we learn about natural disasters from broadcast news? More specifically, what meanings does TV news assign to nature, natural disasters, and the places where they occur? Does TV, by virtue of its unique aesthetic, in fact create natural disaster events for the small screen? How do the inherent qualities of the television medium and the structure of TV news affect the way we understand nature, natural disasters, or the places where they happen? What is the value in trying to understand our relationship to nature and natural disaster as shaped by TV news accounts? These are the general questions explored in this book.

Constructing the Heartland uses TV news coverage of the 1993 midwest flood and, to a lesser degree, the 1997 midwest flood as case studies to analyze the intersection of TV, news, and nature, with specific focus on how all of these must be examined within the context of place. The first part of the inquiry here is the quality of natural disaster news on TV. More specifically, how the medium of TV—its technology and aesthetic—as well as the formulas of TV news shape our views of nature and what we call natural disaster. Second, the study focuses on how nature is viewed or perceived through the context of place in popular culture, and on TV in particular. The three cultural domains of interest—news, nature, and place—are examined from a theoretical framework that combines ideas from cultural geography, media ecology, and TV aesthetics.

Cultural geography concerns itself with the ways in which culture both constructs and is constructed by geographic places (Burgess & Gold, 1985; Duncan & Ley, 1993). The content of mass media, TV news in particular, is an active site for place construction, representation, and meaning. However, in addition to examining content, it is also important to examine the form of TV. The medium has a profound impact on our conceptions and understandings of place and nature. We live in an age dominated by electronic media, which alter our sense perceptions and create a culture and perceptual environment quite different from the environments of print-dominant culture. A media ecology perspective, as articulated initially in the ideas of Harold Innis, Marshall McLuhan, Walter Ong, and others, contrasts the biases of oral, print-based, and electronic media-based cultures.

Regarding electronic media, there are two strains of thought in media ecology. The first strain is represented in the ideas of McLuhan and Ong, for example, who argued the acoustic versus visual biases of media as they dominate in different cultural eras. What traditional oral and contemporary electronic media-based cultures share is a bias toward the ear—an acoustic bias even in image-based electronic media such as TV. Print-based culture, which is situated historically between oral-based and electronic media-based culture, is visually biased, referring to the abstract visualism of the printed word. Media ecology concerns itself with understanding the different social environments created by different media of communication because of their distinct biases. These social environments include the ways of thinking about, relating to, and understanding the world. Because of the inherently different biases of each medium, the social environment created in print-based culture varies greatly from the social environment created in electronic media-based culture. The acoustic bias of TV, an audiovisual medium, is in large part because of its instantaneous speed and global reach. Of course, TV is also inherently recognized as a medium of visual images.

This fact leads to the second strain in media ecology, which is a focus on the revolution of visual images in communications media, specifically the ways in which communication technologies affect image reproduction and image reception—in short, the whole image environment. The significance of the revolution in visual images production can be traced in a number of key scholarly works. Frankfurt School theorist Walter Benjamin's (1968) essay "The Work of Art in the Age of Mechanical Reproduction" details how still images in photographs and moving images on film have had a profound impact on society and collective consciousness. That basic argument is extended in the work of Boorstin (1972), who associated American culture specifically with media formats and discussed the importance of TV specifically to an increased emphasis on image. Postman (1985) continued the discussion in his argument about TV, the medium of images, and how it has negatively shaped public discourse ever increasingly toward entertainment. A focus on the revolution and significance of visual images in communication media is particularly relevant to this book because TV is the medium of primary concern.

The core ideas from media ecology as they concern electronic media generally and TV in particular are revisited throughout this book. They have been expanded on in the work of scholars such as Joshua Meyrowitz and James Carey. In his book *No Sense of Place*, Meyrowitz (1985), outlined his medium theory, which focuses on how electronic media, and TV in particular, alter previously established patterns of access to information. Social changes, he argued, coincide with changes in dominant forms of communication. Electronic media bypass traditional boundaries, specifically those established and maintained in a print-based age, and give us a new world to view and access. Carey (1988) outlined his ritual view of communication in his book *Communication as Culture*, where he argued that cultural studies should be a study of the processes of communication, and particularly communication as the process through which society is created, maintained, and transformed. Carey, like Meyrowitz, contended that emphasis should be placed on the medium, the form of communication. Within the media ecology view, human perceptions of nature and place are quite different in electronic-mediated culture than they were in typographic or print-based culture. The guiding theoretical framework of this study is based in Carey's ritual view of communication and

Meyrowitz's medium theory. Emphasis is placed on the form of communication and the way in which TV in particular—technologically, aesthetically, and ideologically—makes meaning in the world.

Finally, a look at the aesthetic requirements and aesthetic potential of TV brings together the content- and medium-based emphases here. Particularly instructive in this vein is the work of Zettl (1981, 1990, 1998) who focused on TV as a visual, aesthetic medium and who also examined TV's impact as a form of communication. Zettl, who understands the necessity of examining the medium as a whole, focused on how it can be used most effectively. His work comments on the conventions of visual images even as he offers specific instructions about how to create visual images within and beyond those conventions.

In conjunction with the broad theoretical framework just described, this study also combines the concepts *place, regionalism, national identity*, and *nature* to construct a critical framework (Foss, 1989) for analyzing TV as a rhetorical form and a technology. Examining natural disaster coverage generally, and midwest flood coverage specifically, within a theoretical framework that draws on critical cultural geography, media ecology, and television aesthetics, one can begin to understand how and why TV imprints nature and place with its own image production aesthetic and unique logic, thus shaping our understanding as well as our experience of nature and place.

Constructing the Heartland explores the ways in which contemporary TV news accounts of natural disaster borrow from, alter, and extend conceptions of nature as bound within certain geographic and electronic parameters. Natural disasters such as the midwest floods are considered news because they possess news values such as drama and consequence, to name only two. Yet TV does not just capture drama. TV news creates drama in the way language is employed; the way subjects, images, camera shots, and computer graphics are chosen; and the way sequences are edited together. The choices made in presenting as news the 1993 and 1997 midwest floods depended on journalistic *and* aesthetic traditions and conventions. Those choices reinforced nationally shared dominant myths about the regional midwest and the Mississippi River, which have specific and powerful connotations in the national collective imagination or national identity. *National identity*, an ambiguous and contested concept, is defined here as the culmination of historic, economic, and cultural events and practices which are widely shared and which reside in the national memory (Schlesinger, 1991; see also chap. 3, this volume). These events and practices appear in various cultural domains, including on TV. In the case of the 1993 flood, for example, network and local broadcast news told the story of an angry flooding river threatening the relatively peaceful lives of hard-working midwesterners who, determined to win a war with the rivers, battled long and hard, seeking the help of the entire community and trusting that God was looking out for their best interest. Although this is a broad generalization and simplification of flood news, it captures the essence of the content of most TV flood news stories. Television's electronic maneuverings—that is, its ability to create pictures and tell a story in a way unlike any other medium—shaped flood news content to fit its own particular style. The end result was news from the midwest that corroborated, even as it altered, historic, nationally shared notions about defining characteristics of the midwest heartland, the mighty Mississippi River, and even the nation. Coverage of the 1993 and 1997 floods exemplified the unique way in which nature in the midwest is conceived of, interpreted, and presented on TV.

Analysis of flood news includes an examination of reports from the three major broadcast networks and local flood reports from affiliate stations in Des Moines, Iowa; Davenport, Iowa/Rock Island, Illinois; St. Louis, Missouri; and Minneapolis/St. Paul, Minnesota. Included are interviews with local and network reporters, and with network news graphics personnel. Due to resource constraints, only the three major broadcast networks are included here, although CNN and other TV news outlets extensively covered both floods. Altogether flood data include analysis of 248 ABC, CBS, and NBC daily news stories; roughly 37 VHS tapes filled with back-to-back local daily news stories archived at the prior network affiliates; and approximately 11 compilations tapes of flood coverage produced by the local stations and by national producers such as PBS, ABC's *Nightline*, National Geographic Explorer, the Army Corps of Engineers, and the Federal Emergency Management Association (FEMA). Discussion and analysis of this video coverage is based primarily on qualitative analysis. However, to manage the large number of news stories, quantitative content analysis was used to establish patterns of coverage, particularly the use of certain news frames, terms for the flood, and midwest iconography. Qualitative analysis, the predominant methodology of this study, is employed to closely analyze select news stories, compilation tapes and interviews with news personnel, and to draw conclusions about the meanings and significance of TV flood news from and about the midwest. Combining quantitative and qualitative methods allows one to break through traditional methodological barriers and recognize the strengths of both approaches in helping one discover the underlying patterns and meanings in televised news of events such as the floods. Sociologist Alford (1998) argued that, "Developing paradigms of inquiry that recognize historical processes, symbolic meanings and multivariate relations is the best way to construct an adequate explanation of a complex social phenomenon" (p. 19).

The midwest floods occurred within a broad historical and spatial context. Discourses of the midwest, its iconography, and its significance within the larger nation's culture and identity require that flood news be situated on an appropriate time/space continuum. Therefore, in addition to the primary data—the flood news—and in an attempt to place the representations and meanings surrounding the flood in a broader, historical context, included here are discussions about factual and fictional literary accounts of the midwest and the Mississippi River. These include Mark Twain's *Life on the Mississippi*; Barry's (1997) *Rising Tide*, which looks at the Mississippi Flood of 1927 and how it changed the nation; and short stories and other literary accounts of the midwest produced by many other writers including Willa Cather, Bill Holm, and others. Also important to establishing the context are discussions and examinations of other artistic representations such as those by painters Grant Wood and John Bloom and filmmaker Pare Lorentz. Sources such as these establish historic precedent, demonstrate the rich lore, and exemplify the various media from which myths of nature and the region emerge and circulate. Contemporary representations of the midwest, including TV news, draw from this cultural lore. Yet because of the unique way in which TV delivers images and places, the way it creates virtual environments, televisual codes and our understanding of them alter these representations. This study examines how journalists draw on collective ideals of nature and place, but also explores how the technology of TV and the contingencies of the broadcast infrastructure as a whole alter or reshape those ideals.

Exploring both the content and form of TV, as this book does, reveals the complexity of the medium and its relationship to social life and culture broadly. As Zettl (1998) explained, "After all, it is not just content alone or form alone that shapes our media experience, but the synthesis of both" (p. 84). In that vein, some media scholars have explored the complexity of TV with its tendency toward simultaneous continuity and change, whereas others have focused specifically on how TV alters our relationship to the world and each other. Silverstone (1988) argued that TV presents the content of myth while creating by its technology "a distinct spatial and temporal environment marked by the screen and marking for all to see the tissue boundary between the profane and the sacred" (p. 29). Likewise, Carey (1988) argued that TV both perpetuates culture through myth-repairing narratives and changes culture through technology that transcends space and time. Meyrowitz (1998) offered a useful analytical tool for examining both form and content. His concept of multiple media literacies suggests that media literacy and analysis requires that one understand: (a) content literacy, (b) grammar literacy (an understanding of basic production aesthetics), and

(c) medium literacy—an understanding of how TV as a medium positions and directs us. This three-part way of understanding and analyzing television can easily and usefully be applied to TV natural disaster news, and this study attempts to accomplish that.

Because of TV's unique capacity to electronically deliver sound, images, and other effects to a nation, even world, of viewers simultaneously, TV news has nearly supplanted print news as the most relied on and trusted sources of information. Although other electronic media, computer-based media and the Internet specifically are fast becoming important sources of news and information, TV still matters. It is TV news above other news sources that, in many places, still dominates. This study discusses the implications of producing and sending images of disaster from one place to a geographically dispersend audience, attending to the ways in which our conceptions of natural disasters and the places where they happen are shaped by immediate and oftentimes constant dramatic imagery, unlike the way in which we receive such information via print news. By way of exploring the social constructions wrought by television news agents and technology, the study asks: What is the nature of televised information, and how does that affect TV news about nature's obstructions, particularly in specifically identified places? How and why do reporters and news executives make the decisions they do to use particular visuals and types of language to report natural disasters? What are the implications? In broader terms, how are conceptions of natural disaster and places altered by changes in communications media?

Considered here are the following broad theoretical questions, listed in order of philosophical and practical relevance to this study: What sort of nature representations do we consider appropriate? To what extent, and under what circumstances, do we separate nature from culture or human activity? How are our representations of nature tied to specific geographic places? In light of these, the more focused theoretical questions is: How does TV news as a cultural form, cultural practice, and unique medium draw on, extend, and/or alter our understandings about nature and place when reporting what we have come to call *natural disasters*? On a more empirical level: What role did broadcast journalism play in responding to the heavy flooding in the midwest in 1993 and 1997? Through what strategies did TV news act to repair nature and its damages, and to maintain midwest identity through flood reporting? How were the strategies, technologies, infrastructure, format, and personnel of TV news relevant to such repair? In what ways, and why, did national news differ from local news?

To illustrate some of the areas of focus in the study, the following are brief discussions of two aspects of flood coverage—news frames and videotaped flood commemorations. Essentially both floods were covered as instances where nature was out of control and the defining characteristics of the heartland were challenged as they were brought into national focus. In classic studies of the news, both Gans (1979) and Tuchman (1978) described the ways in which the press routinely place they own structure on otherwise unstructured events, giving them legitimating frames of reference through which we understand the world. During the flood, by adopting certain news frames, broadcast news attempted to make sense of the continuous flooding while working diligently to repair and restore the idyllic heartland myth. One general way in which the news attempted to understand the flood was to cast it in terms of victimizer and victims. A prevailing war metaphor was employed throughout flood coverage on both local and network levels. According to TV news, the battles on the Mississippi River were waged between farmers and townsfolk who had worked hard to build successful farms and family businesses, only to see nature willfully work to destroy all they had achieved. In the struggle for economic and human survival, midwesterners pulled together, fighting the river with sandbags and through other means, sometimes to no avail. Despite small victories here and there, and despite the community's hard work, nature often won in the end, but the community remained solid. Studying news frames at work in TV news means looking not only at the ideological frames such as the war metaphor, but the aesthetic frame as well.

This includes looking at how camera use, graphics, editing techniques, and other special effects together offered viewers an incredible sensual and dramatic experience of the flood. Because TV is visual above all, the aesthetic frame was perhaps the overaching frame through which other news frames were employed. Heavy use of the aesthetic news frame was a powerful strategy used by the networks to understand the disaster and repair the heartland myth. Yet beyond immediate efforts of news personnel, the heartland myth was already altered by televisual logic to conform to the demands of the medium and corroborate its acoustic bias.

In addition to examining news frames, this study also looks at a unique aspect of both the 1993 and 1997 floods—one that cannot be separated from the daily TV news coverage. Specifically, it is the way in which the floods were and are locally commemorated. Many local TV stations developed compilation tapes of the *best of* flood coverage, most immediately after the fact, and sold them in local retail outlets as keepsakes—a way for residents of flood-ravaged areas to remember the flood and their struggles during that time. These compilation tapes or commemorations were highly structured narratives wherein the local TV station(s), acting as cultural historians and archivists, worked to melodramatically reconstruct the flood events for the public memory while promoting themselves and their own heroic efforts during the floods. Along with local commemoration tapes are examinations of other popular culture aspects of the floods, including annual community events, ballads, displays, performances, and clothing items and other commodities. These localized popular culture items are borne of similar impulses driving television news coverage generally: the desire to assign meaning to the flood, identify heroes and victims, achieve economic gain, and explain the chaos of nature in cultural terms, and specifically in terms that make sense in electronic media-based culture.

BEYOND THE FLOOD

The Great Flood of 1993 and the 1997 midwest flood are just two among many, many national and international natural disasters broadcast repeatedly on TV. The core questions concerning communications media and representations of nature and place are relevant beyond the flood stories. Examining myths of nature and place generally, and how TV news draws on and extends, yet alters, them is a useful way in which to analyze news about earthquakes, hurricanes, and a host of other natural disasters and environmental phenomena as they unfold in other regions of the United States, other cities, other states, and other parts of the world. *Place* is an important context to consider when examining our conceptions and televised representations of nature, particularly nature's obstructions. One could ask: What meanings does TV news assign to earthquakes in other regions of the country? In other nations? What meanings and significance underlie TV news reports of forest fires in the northwest? The south? Are mythic ways of thinking about these regions relevant to the ways in which TV news frames the activities of nature unfolding there? What about television news from U.S. sources about natural disasters in other parts of the world? Much has been written about the predominance of disaster news from lesser developed countries (Adams, 1986; Gaddy & Tanjong, 1986; Rosenblum, 1970). Although most of these focus chiefly on quantity of coverage, and look at both print and broadcast news, what is proposed here is that we examine the quality of TV news specifically. Can we enhance our understanding of the ideologies imposed on places geographically and culturally removed from the United States by examining the news frames, the metaphors and the myths employed in natural disaster TV news coverage from those places? This question precludes a specific theoretical framework within which to examine natural disaster and environmental news on TV not only within the United States but elsewhere. The prima-

ry focus of analysis of all such coverage should be nature representations within the context of place meaning, as a product of TV specifically, and of the biases of electronic media generally. These cannot be separated. It is important to examine TV as a mythic force or active agent in
presentation and alterations of myths, nature representations, and place
meanings. Understanding TV news content and technology—from critical, aesthetic, and media ecology perspectives—leads to a better understanding of the complexity of the broad geography of natural disaster
reporting on TV.

BRIEF CHAPTER DESCRIPTIONS

The book is divided into seven chapters, including this introductory
chapter. Chapter 1, "*Nature, Place, and Television News*," outlines the
study, constructs the theoretical framework for analysis, and provides a
rationale for examining nature in place via natural disaster TV news
coverage. Included in chapter 1 are relevant concepts and areas of study
from cultural geography and media studies, specifically media ecology,
TV aesthetics, and TV news. The chapter examines the discourses of
nature, cultural place construction, TV as a mythic force, TV as technology and news as narrative practice.

Chapter 2, "*The Heartland Myth: Region, Nation, and Geographic
Identity*," outlines the significance and meaning of the heartland myth
and of regional identity as part of the larger national identity. The chapter explores regional difference and midwest regional representations,
and includes a close analysis of flood news stories that draws from the
historic precedent of the midwest agrarian myth. Chapter 2 includes a
discussion of the historic settlement of the midwest, the history of intervention on the Mississippi River, the myth and realities of agricultural
life and how the midwest has been portrayed in various media.

Chapter 3, "*Landscapes of Disaster: Visual Aesthetics of Flood
News*," focuses on how the larger cultural practices of framing nature are
evident in TV news format and technology. In particular, the chapter
closely examines how such aesthetic production practices as camera use,
editing, helicopters and other technologies, and the entire apparatus of
TV are all part of myth perpetuation, alteration and repair in TV news
coverage through the creation of what are called *landscapes of disaster*.
Chapter 3 also examines how other visual elements in the news—the
maps and other graphics used during flood coverage—are significant in
ideologically placing the story in context. Such visuals add important
information to disaster stories, thus helping to create the drama by
enhancing news frames and imposing their own ideological context. A

brief discussion of cartography sets up the historical context for our contemporary understanding of maps as representations of place, as conduits for visualizing places from various frames of reference, and how news cartography especially has helped shape our geographic understanding. Also included is a discussion of the use of still store images and of the insight gleaned from interviews with several network directors of news graphics who offer a sense of how decisions are made about which images to use and where they are to be placed within the story.

Chapter 4, "*Local Versus National Flood News*," is a comparison of stories on the local level with network stories to determine how journalists carry out their journalistic duty during natural disaster situations. A discussion of television news ethics questions the concept of journalistic duty and news ethics generally within the medium of TV. Chapter 4 also includes interviews with local and network reporters who discuss how they perceived their role in flood coverage.

Chapter 5, "*Television Flood Commemoration and Popular Culture*," emphasizes predominantly the videotapes and compiled *best of* footage produced by local TV stations and national producers to commemorate the awesome floods as horrific spectacles. The flood special videotapes, particularly those produced by local affiliate stations, were compiled immediately after the worst of the flooding within the area. Each is a chronological account employing the most highly dramatic coverage with added music, effects, and graphics. Most were originally sold in local retail establishments as mementos of the flood and to raise money to aid local victims. The flood specials—unique narratives of flood devastation and control—both glorified the work of the local news teams who compiled them and continue to serve as archives of history and folklore for the local area, commemorating the momentous conflict and work of the community in restoring the flooded river to its more appropriate peaceful state, where it could continue its service to residents on the flood plain. Chapter 5 also discusses other popular culture flood outcomes such as ballads written about the flood, flood t-shirts and other commodities that sprang from the flood, and other exhibits and performances inspired by these natural disasters. These also add to the cultural history of the floods and exemplify, on the one hand, the extent to which the flood has contributed to place myth and meaning, and on the other, the extent to which the medium of TV has shaped the collective memory of the floods. The end of the chapter includes a discussion of other televised natural disasters, both fiction and nonfiction.

The final chapter, chapter 6, "*Understanding Place, Television News and Natural Disaster*," moves beyond the midwest floods to discuss how the framework for analysis—grounded in critical media studies and media ecology—can be used in a larger context to examine TV news and other natural disasters in other places. The chapter offers a final look at the overarching conclusions drawn from the study, including the relevance of understanding televised representations and conceptions of nature and the environment during a period of increasing forms and use of electronic media as well as increased environmental concerns worldwide. Included is a discussion of possible avenues for further research concerning nature and place in electronic media.

Finally, although the entire study looks critically and analytically at TV's role in the creation of natural disasters, the intent is not to take away from the real losses suffered by many, many people in the midwest during the 1993 and 1997 floods. Those were not created by the medium, but suffered and endured by thousands located in the areas flooded by the Mississippi and Red Rivers and their many tributaries. The aim here is to focus on the political/ideological, historical, and technological dimensions of flood coverage, not on diminishing or dismissing the emotional and material consequences visited on those who lived through and are still living through what happened to them during those years. This study focuses on TV's treatment of what happened. The final goal of this book is that all readers take away a better understanding of how TV news operates within a broad sociocultural context, and that TV news plays a significant role in both shaping and reinforcing reality in our everyday lives.

1

Nature, Place, and
TV News

The July 5th CBS Evening News broadcast opened with the flood story. From the CBS network studio in New York, Connie Chung began the newscast by describing the latest in what she called the *midwest's battle* on the Mississippi River. As she continued reporting about the flood, her image was replaced with a screen filled by a computer-generated globe on which appeared a representation of North America. From there, the image zoomed in to only the United States, then to the center of the nation, and finally to the state of Missouri. As Chung introduced Vickie Mabrey, the CBS correspondent reporting from Missouri, the computer-generated outline of the state flipped; on the other side was the first image in the video footage of the flood in and around West Alton, Missouri.

Mabrey's voiceover accompanied a barrage of images that were part of her flood report for that day. The first image was an extreme long shot of the deluged rural expanse captured by a camera situated high above it in a quickly moving helicopter. The whirring helicopter blades could be heard in the background as Mabrey described the scene unfolding on the screen—many treetops and a few rooftops barely visible above an expanse of water creeping to the horizon. From that height,

15

viewers witnessed the breadth of the flooded Mississippi. Next from the noisy helicopter was a shot of sandbaggers in a farm field, then a long shot from the ground angled up at the sandbaggers. Mabrey explained, over that sequence, that "All of the preparations in the world seem unable to stop a river bent on overstepping its bounds." As Mabrey went on to describe the difficulties and worries of farmers in the area who stood to lose all of their crops, the following images were strung together: a close shot of a farmer in seed cap being interviewed on his tractor as he rode with other farmers and a load of sandbags; a medium close shot of a second farmer standing next to a flooded field describing his losses and his worries; a medium shot of Mabrey speaking to the camera while standing in a farm field; cut back to a medium close shot of farmer number two standing in a less flooded field; then to a moving helicopter shot along the flooded town of Grafton, Illinois; to a helicopter shot of flooded Davenport, Iowa; to a helicopter shot of a small levee, with a zoom to an American flag stuck between sandbags. Mabrey explained over these images details of current damages in these areas and how residents were living in fear of even more. Next viewers saw an extreme close shot of the man who built the flag-bearing levee and heard him explain, in a faint, quivering voice, that he has always had a lot of respect for the river, and, although he is hoping he will beat it this time, he does not have much hope. The final image was a helicopter shot of rural Davenport, with the camera angled down on two people walking in floodwaters, then a zoom out to the expanse of flood in the area. A shadow of the moving helicopter was visible on screen as it whirred just below Mabrey's closing comments.

The entire fast-paced story—2 minutes, 20 seconds long—included 31 different images. The major themes of the report were the power of the river, the plight of the farmers, and the altered midwest landscape. These themes were executed in a tightly packaged, fast-paced sequence of images that focused on movement: within shots, between shots, and by the camera as it traveled from sky to ground and back again. Those watching the report on their TV sets were literally flooded with an array of audiovisual elements not unusual for dramatic TV news stories, and certainly not unlike most of the flood coverage on all three major networks during that summer.

Long after the 1993 flood had receded, CBS revisited it, this time in an episode of their *I Remember* series hosted by Charles Kuralt. The series featured major events of the recent past. The flood episode, which aired on May 22, 1997, was essentially a view of the flood from the perspectives of three of the CBS correspondents sent to cover it in 1993: Vickie Mabrey, Harry Smith, and Bob Orr. Kuralt introduced the episode saying the Mississippi River just could not be tamed. He also spoke about rains of Biblical proportions that were responsible for the river's overflow. Each segment of the half-hour program was narrated from a studio by the three correspondents. Each was shot at medium and medium close length as they spoke to an invisible party off-screen. The images of the correspondents were interspersed with cutaways to images of the flood, some of which had been part of their own individual packages and some supplemental images shot at the time, but not used in the original broadcasts. The correspondents described what it was like for them to cover the flood, offering a behind-the-scenes look at the hardships and emotions they had experienced while reporting on what each called a disaster the likes of which they had never before seen. The three recalled being awestruck and impressed while witnessing and reporting on the midwest disaster.

Helicopters figured prominently in the footage featured in this episode and in the correspondents' own renderings of daily procedures for flood coverage. For all three reporters, the helicopter was an essential tool of newsgathering and broadcasting. In Mabrey's animated description of the flood, she indicated a particular moment during coverage that was aided by helicopter and that encapsulated the flood. That moment was the utter dismantling of a farmhouse just outside St. Louis on August 1, when one of the levees holding back the Mississippi River finally gave way. Mabrey described the dismantled structure as the quintessential turn-of-the-century white farmhouse. As she explained what happened to it, a camera in a helicopter lingered on images of the crumbling farmhouse and farm buildings—the same footage CBS used in its coverage on that day in 1993. The threefold focus in this CBS retrospective, besides the reporters, was the power of the river, the plight of the people, and the transformed midwest landscape.

The two news pieces described previously are different in some ways, but in other ways they are much the same. The first is an example of daily network coverage as the flood unfolded, the second a look back long after the flood ceased to be a network news item. The July 5th story is purportedly a dispassionate correspondent package, whereas the *I Remember* piece is a view from three correspondents as intimately involved and personally affected. However, both are visually alluring, fast-paced, emotionally charged, formulaic TV news pieces. Both relied on the same kinds of footage and employed familiar TV news techniques, including introductions from the studio and cutaways to the locale of the story. Both also made use of TV's aural and visual technologies, such as sophisticated editing equipment and techniques, computer graphics, sound effects, and helicopters for transport and extremely high angle camera shots. Because of the time allowed to develop it, the second piece added sound and visual effects in a more obvious and deliberate fashion than did the first, but it was more a matter of degree than overall impact.

In addition to their similarities in visual format and technology, both pieces were ideologically similar. Both recounted the drama of man versus nature and, more specifically, the river versus the midwest farmers and communities. The underlying themes in both pieces were the power of the river, how that power was overcoming or had overcome midwesterners, and how the midwest landscape was transforming or had been transformed because of the flood. Broadly speaking, these were the dominant underlying themes of *all* of the TV coverage of the midwest flood of 1993: the local, network, documentary, and retrospective coverage. Understanding how and why those themes or meanings were manifest, the forms they took in TV news, and how they developed over time requires first an understanding of the connections among nature, place, and TV.

Nature, place, and the medium of TV are equally relevant in TV natural disaster news. The complex medium of TV creates, re-creates, and transforms our understanding of nature and place. Television's complexity lies in content, in technology, and aesthetics. These three are not mutually exclusive, but are intertwined. Any comprehensive discussion of the medium must consider *what* it says, *how* it says it, and by *what means* these messages are created, transmitted, understood, and reverberated in time and space. Put more simply, TV is more than content, and it is more than technology. It is a way of conceiving of and understanding a culture within which it is embedded and of which it has partially created. Although the term *culture* can be broad, complex, and variously defined (see Dirks, Eley, & Ortner, 1994), here it is defined as the complex circulation of discourses, representations, and meanings in everyday life. These are sometimes shared, oftentimes contested. Of particular concern here are discourses about and meanings of nature and place, specifically on TV.

Instances of televised natural disaster news coverage are ideal opportunities to examine our cultural discourses and representations of nature and place. Disasters are those occasions where nature seems to have overstepped the cultural bounds we have constructed. Nature becomes, in anthropologist Douglas' (1966) term, *matter out of place*. TV news disaster reports are also opportunities to better understand how TV has partly shaped and continues to shape our understanding of nature and place. The news stories described at the beginning of the chapter are neither exceptional nor unique in the way they reported on the flood, but they are instructive examples of the ways in which TV news delineates a natural disaster and the place where it occurs. They are also instructive examples of how TV news creates and shapes both.

NATURE

An enormous, all-encompassing, and almost confusing concept, nature can be coopted for almost any purpose and can mean many different things depending on the context of its usage. Certainly to try to define nature is futile, so fraught is it with human cultural baggage, so layered in human practice and symbolic representation, and so encumbered by history. Common forms of usage are in discussions and analyses of human nature, the natural world, the natural environment, and/or that which exists beyond our planet. The position taken here is that nature is not a raw entity separate from culture or human activity. It is not somehow beyond culture; it is interconnected with culture. We understand it through our discourses and systems of representation, and indeed we function as organic (or partially organic in some instances) beings in environments where the organic is situated next to and with the built or constructed. Rather than spend time arguing about what nature is, it is more fruitful to look historically and culturally at the development of ideas about nature, the ways in which it has been and is regarded, controlled, represented, and/or discussed. A cultural/historic look offers a better understanding of our present-day and possibly even future thoughts and actions.

Examining the concept of nature, past and present, is a daunting task to say the least, but a look at research and writing about nature reveals a number of clear contexts for thinking about or explaining it. These contexts, diverse, but by no means exhaustive, are: myth, religion, economics, politics, and identity. Each context offers a different framework for understanding how nature has been conceptualized and used, both physically and theoretically. What these contexts have in common is that all of them, of necessity, identify nature in terms of human endeavor and within human value systems.

Those who have written about views of nature in early times trace them either to tribal societies, specific ancient Western societies such as early Greeks, or western mythology generally. Burch (1984) described tribal societies as those engaged in "Enchanted exploitation of nature where they talk to animals and plants and seek their help in survival and personal problems" (p. 10). Burch contrasted this with the ancient Greeks who, according to Kelsen (1946), treated nature and society as quite different entities. Torrance (1992) also examined the concept of nature in Greek antiquity, arguing that one cannot make generalizations about the Greek view of nature. He explained that for some it was sharply contrasted with culture or the world of law, custom, and social codes. For other Greeks it was permeated with values and was a resource for moral philosophizing. Nature or the natural was used, in those cases, to legitimate a point of view specific to the interests of certain groups. In other words, nature changed meaning depending on the circumstance and what was at stake. One point Torrance clearly made in his book is that the Greeks were not driven to study nature to control it or appropriate it. Although it was not clearly defined, it was, for the Greeks of antiquity, an entity conceived of within the parameters of culture.

Historian Schama (1995) discussed nature specifically in terms of landscape or nature as visually contained. His interest lies in historic and contemporary presentations of nature as scenery and as held in memory. Schama's analysis of the meanings of natural landscapes includes a look at early Western nature myths, including the myth of Arcadia and Pan's fertile realm. He traced early myths of wood, water, and rock, offering an exhaustive account of where and by whom these myths generated, and how they have held fast. These myths, he argued, informed the landscapes later created in paintings and photography and still shape the way we think about nature and natural landscapes. In his work, Schama was not interested in defining *nature*, but instead in discussing how early Western myths of nature are retained in our conception of appropriate landscapes, and to make connections between landscapes and national identity—a connection and discussion more fully developed in chapter 3 of this book.

Geographer and theorist Harvey (1996) offered a broad historical-geographic-economic look at nature or the natural environment. Harvey delineated specifically the European Enlightenment period as the source of much of our contemporary understanding of nature. Individual emancipation, secularism, and scientific rationalism are key ideas or constructs introduced during the Enlightenment. Emancipation and self-realization, Harvey explained, were thought to be contingent on the human capacity to dominate nature. The domination thesis, espoused by Bacon, Descartes, Leibniz, Spinoza, and others, offered individuals and groups, via scientific reason and the scientific method, the power to shape life. According to Harvey, in capitalism we are still bound by this thesis. Likewise, but more specifically, historian Steinberg (2000) focused on nature as property. The American penchant for owning nature, he argued, shows how absurd life in the modern world has become. However, he wrote, "The natural world's continued resistance to human meddling suggests the weakness of a system of thought that centers so thoroughly on possession" (p. 10).

Working in tandem with the capitalist imperative is the Christian. Harvey suggested that the Enlightenment domination thesis was ideologically rooted in Christianity. Geographers Seymour and Watkins (1995) pointed out Protestantism in particular as advocating nature domination. In Protestant Christianity, they argued, there is an absence of nature deities and a poorly developed sense of nature as sacred in itself perhaps because of the promise of an eternal life in another world. However, the Protestant version of the domination thesis has changed slightly, in keeping with more recent broad sociopolitical concerns about the environment. Since the 1970s, Protestant theology generally has placed more emphasis on good stewardship of the land as opposed to strict domination. In his book *Imagined Country: Society, Culture, and Environment*, Short (1991) cautioned against oversimplification of Christian nature views. Different factions within the larger Christian tradition have in the past, and even today, held differing views. Some espouse safeguarding the land, whereas others advocate domination of the land as, they argued, God intended (Barcott, 2001).

In contrast to Christian views, Eastern religions such as Taoism, Buddhism, and Hinduism offer other views of nature. Although there are vast differences among these three religions, what they share is a belief in the unity of the world—that all things are one. In his book *Nature's Web*, Marshall (1994) discussed the relationship between humans and the natural world from many different religious perspectives. As Marshall explained, Taoists believe one should submit to natural processes and never work against them. Nature constantly strives for equilibrium. Taoists stress that the causes of social conflict and natural disaster are to be found in human domination and hierarchy. Buddhism stresses compassion for all beings because life is one and indivisible. Humans try to separate themselves from nature, but they are still a part of nature. The Hindu religion encourages compassion for all creatures. Vedas are Hindu hymns to the earth and in celebration of the mysteries of the universe. Hindu Yogis seek the wilderness and other desolate regions to discover ultimate reality, while the masses travel to rivers, the source and support of spiritual life, and the symbol of life without end.

A compelling example of culturally opposing views of nature is that offered by Dietrich (1995) in his grand historic narrative of the altered Columbia River in the western United States. American Indians, he wrote, saw the river as a generous larder, whereas to White entrepreneurs and boosters it was a source for electricity, agriculture, and wealth. The present-day Columbia River, with its dams, altered terrain, and ecological fragility, reveals how one set of meanings or conceptions of the river overrode another.

Traditional Native American beliefs, although not identical across tribes and nations, regard nature as sacred. Generally, within this broad set of beliefs, one lives according to an understanding of harmony among people, animals, water, elements, flora, and deities. Contemporary New Age religions, or countercultures, have taken some of these traditional beliefs and married them to a contemporary environmental consciousness as well as a contemporary consumer lifestyle. For the most part, this resurgent religious interest in nature and the environment among non-natives coincides with a general recognition of the rampant anti-environmental excesses of capitalism and industrialization in the last two centuries. However, a certain irony exists in our current exultation of nature. We openly espouse its sacred qualities while not giving up the excesses that threaten to choke it out. Nature is often a separate space set apart from the places where we typically live, drive, and generally consume. National parks and native preserves are sectioned off for occasional respite from the rest of the world. Yet, we destroy the environment on our way to revere and celebrate sacred nature. Automobiles, motorized boats, and other fuel-burning vehicles put in danger the very elements, living and nonliving, we claim to herald. Another irony of this mindset is the way nature is revered as image. Print ads and TV commercials include nature images as backdrops to any number of consumer goods. The idea of nature as sacred is trendy, sophisticated even, but it is not a whole way of living. It is a separate category—one we have defined.

Despite changes through time, the contexts discussed earlier all assume at their foundation, sometimes implicitly, that nature is not completely separate from culture. Certainly it is defined in cultural terms. Geographer Larsen (1992) quite explicitly claimed that, in the past as well as today, nature serves functions that are aesthetic, political, economic, and ethical. We use nature, he argued, for political, economic, and aesthetic purposes, and so on. We conceive of nature much like we do other cultural texts and artifacts. In other words, we cannot conceptualize nature outside the frameworks we use to conceptualize or understand other phenomena of our everyday experience.

Nature, or the natural as we understand it, is dependent on the social. The form of this dependence has been examined by various scholars throughout the social sciences. Some analyze how perspectives on nature have changed historically (Cartwill, 1993) and, like Harvey, how capitalism dominates nature and situates it within the political-economic order (Gitlin, 1987). Cultural geographers have examined the enculturation of nature by looking at the way landscapes and other geographic spaces are defined through descriptive practices or discourses that change in time (see Daniels & Cosgrove, 1993). Haraway (1989) argued that the themes of race, sexuality, gender, nation, family, and class have all been written into the body of nature in Western life sciences since the 18th century. Accordingto Haraway, nature is a deeply contested myth and reality. Consequently, we view nature as a force, setting, and/or phenomenon that can be either positive or negative depending on how it is situated vis-à-vis human activity. Short (1991) explained that two prevailing views of nature have persisted in Western thought. One is the Romantic view, or nature as spiritual paradise. The other is the Classical view, or nature and wilderness as that which must be feared and overcome.

Leeson (1994) explained that nature is conceived of simultaneously as friend and foe. He assessed the way two sides of the environmental debate have manufactured images of nature to reinforce their own arguments. Both views highlight the natural world's ability to inspire awe and fear. According to Leeson, the industry view of nature is as a resource, utility, or employee; that is, nature is constructed as a force to be dominated because it is a source of both wealth and destruction. However, environmental activists often construct nature as victimized Eden, friend, and, although object of fear, not to be contained because its sheer power renders it a source of human peak experiences. Both arguments, veering either to the Romantic or Classical view, place nature within the realm of the social, and as a social entity nature is assumed to possess human characteristics, including the capacity for fairness and reason. Leeson explained that Locke's theory of the social contract has come to include nature and, he argued, "when the deal goes sour, we're bewildered . . . nature violates the paradigms in which we attempt to contain it" (p. 41).

Because *nature* is defined in sociocultural terms, it is not available to us as raw, objective reality apart from human activity or understanding. To define it as separate reifies the nature–culture split in structural theory. Levi-Strauss (1966) argued such distinction is a universal means to understanding because it is basic to the structure of the mind. However, challenges to structuralist thinking exist. The nature–culture dichotomy can be considered simplistic at the least. Some argue that humans are part of the natural world and can experience it outside the confines of symbolic representation (see Slack, 1996). However, nature is a construction insofar as humans understand the natural world via the filters of our available symbol systems. Nature is mediated through language and images, and through other existing social categories, including our paradigms of understanding, as Leeson pointed out. Although we might discursively separate nature from ourselves (culture), we persist in appropriating nature into our cultural symbol systems aided by our technologies.

It is clear that no consensus exists where nature is concerned, but the concept or idea is easily evoked. Although we cannot necessarily explain exactly what nature is, it is useful to us as a source of wealth, spirituality, political gain, physical activity, and aesthetic enjoyment, and as a backdrop for our daily activities and pleasures. Television news reports of the 1993 flood used nature—the river and the land—as key elements of drama and of visual spectacle. Embedded in these news reports were assumptions about nature's true purpose, property, and nature as friend as well as foe. In these reports nature was a social construct.

NATURE AND COMMUNICATIONS MEDIA

The contexts discussed earlier provide different frameworks for understanding nature, through time, in human terms. They also provide evidence of the near impossibility of conceiving something like nature apart from human activity or understanding. One context not yet discussed is the context of communications media. Our relationship to and conceptualization of nature must also be examined in terms of the dominant communications medium of an historic era.

McLuhan (1973) argued that different communications technologies create different perceptions of and relationships to nature. McLuhan specifically described the way in which media, as extensions of the body, alter sense ratios and patterns of perception, hence our experience of the world. In early oral culture, humans were more acoustically oriented—dominated by the ear. They were more communal and less individuated. Their relationship with nature was that of interdependence; they did not perceive of a separation between themselves and nature, and chiefly concerned themselves with their immediate surroundings. McLuhan's argument about the human–nature relationship coincides with Burch's description of tribal society as outlined earlier. However, McLuhan explained why the relationship was that way in tribal society. The dominant mode of communications at that time—orality— shaped tribal perceptions and worldviews.

The invention of the alphabet and later of moveable type created a completely different orientation to the world. Print-dominant culture allowed for the creation of larger kingdoms and nation-states. Print, an extension of the eye, made humans visually oriented, leading to perceptions of space and time as continuous and quantifiable. Nature was objectified and perceived as separate from humans or culture and necessarily controllable. Again there is a link between McLuhan's assessment of the invention of print, and especially of moveable type, and what Harvey argued about changes in nature perceptions during the Enlightenment period. The vast social, political, and scientific changes wrought by the Enlightenment coincided with the invention of moveable type, and one can argue that the Enlightenment was possible because of print technology.

Our present culture, dominated by electronic media, is, according to McLuhan, becoming again more acoustically oriented, but in a different way. Ong (1982) uses the term *secondary orality* or *literate orality* to identify the current age of electronic communication. Ong observed that we are once again experiencing elements from the oral age in that our perceptions are becoming again more acoustically oriented, but the new orality is electronically mediated. The sense of tribal harmony experienced in traditional oral societies is now combined with the self-conscious analysis of literacy carried over from the print age. The new orality, because of electronic media's instantaneous speed and global reach, makes possible a different, more accessible environment worldwide. According to McLuhan (1973), with the launch of Sputnik in 1957, "For the first time the natural world was completely enclosed in a man-made container. At the moment that the earth went inside this new artifact, Nature ended and Ecology was born" (p. 49). By ecology, McLuhan was referring to the acoustic orientation or acoustic space created by electronic media wherein human beings seek to maintain equilibrium among environmental components. Television, McLuhan argued, provides instant involvement. Electronic man is able to be everywhere. Regarding nature specifically, McLuhan claimed that electronic media encourage an interdependence with nature, because it is one of the environmental components with which we seek equilibrium.

Extending McLuhan's argument about nature and electronic media-dominated culture, DeLuca (1996) wrote more broadly about technology and the human–nature relationship. Technology transforms one's experience of the world by replacing nature in one's immediate experience. In other words, DeLuca argued, technology is the context of perception. Different technologies help create different perceptions. Like McLuhan, DeLuca explained that oral cultures were more communal, less introspective than literate cultures, and more intimately involved with animate nature. The modern age and its instrumental reason, coinciding with the phonetic alphabet and print, made possible the transformation of practical relations with technology into a technological worldview. In such a view, humans are the subjects—the beings on which all else is grounded. At center stage, humans displace nature. Electronic media, with its acoustic bias, could change that, but, DeLuca argued, may not. He did not agree that electronic communication will necessarily lead to more perceived interdependence with nature because technology is still a part of instrumental reason—an artifact of the Enlightenment. Certainly Ong agreed that although we have entered the age of secondary orality, we have retained what we gained in the print-based or literate age. That is, we have retained a portion of our visual bias and penchant for reason. He cited narrative specifically as an artifact of literate culture. The non-narrative or antinarrative forms of electronic media are responses to literate narrative. Traditional narrative is the standard by which non-narrativity is measured. DeLuca pointed out that suppositions of civility and rationality underlie most mediated representations of nature. These are foundational to the ideographs *progress* and *industrialism*, both of which are borne of the Enlightenment. For example, nature is often depicted as amenable to human interests and activities. Often it is shown in a controlled state or as backdrop to other human activities. When we see nature depicted as *wild*, most often it does not, in those instances, directly threaten humans or human interests. For example, it is fascinating to see footage of an avalanche in a remote mountainous area or of two mountain sheep literally ramming horns in a fight to protect their territory or claim their mate. These can be captured on film or videotape from a safe, secluded distance. In cases such as these, nature's unpredictability or chaos serves an aesthetic, even entertainment function. These would not be considered news per se.

The flood and other natural disasters that threaten human activity are news. They are instances of nature as *un*reasonable in human terms. Especially when they inconvenience us or cost us money, they are perceived as instances of nature out of control. Television encourages such a perspective because of the way it routinely portrays natural disasters. TV news reports are products of corporate media formats, and only a few people actually have access to TV news production. Corporate-run electronic media are part of a larger media system, and that system is responsible for producing images about nature. DeLuca offered an interesting assessment of current tactics used by environmental protest groups such as Greenpeace. The immediacy, imagery, and spectacle of staged protests by groups like Greenpeace—individuals tying themselves to trees, and so on—are attempts to use the potential of the medium to produce other images of nature, expose rational control, and counter the instrumental reason embedded in most televised nature depictions. Electronic media attempt to exert control over nature within rational contexts. Yet it is possible that electronic media could also offer images of nature in other, less controlled contexts. The closest TV comes to this is when, as during the flood, nature is depicted as spectacle.

Television produces images appropriate to the event and in keeping with expectations that have been defined by TV to begin with. In other words, technological advances in visual communications media, from the still images of photography to the moving images of film and video, produce their own sets of expectation. As Boorstin (1972) explained, TV encourages image events, or what he calls *pseudoevents*, because the camera seeks dramatic pictures. In many instances, events are created specifically for the camera. Further, this medium of images, according to Postman (1985), requires a continuously entertaining format. Television, by way of the revolution in image production, has set the bar. It has "made entertainment the natural format for the representation of all experience" (p. 87). We expect visual drama, and heightened experience in the world because of TV. Natural disasters are events that, by TV's standards and our expectations, are made for TV. They are the raw material of nature made perfect in their electronic representation and recontextualization.

Clearly, electronic media offer us greater access to nature, but in a way defined specifically by those media. We can now see and experience things never-before possible without the aid of cameras, computers, and accompanying technologies. Consider that we have relatively easy access to televised undersea explorations and close-up, time-elapsed moving images of blooming flowers. We are also able to witness a live human fetus in-utero. These images are readily available on TV, in videotaped or filmed format, or in digital, computerized format. Because of computers, we can follow mountain climbers and Arctic explorers, step by step, as they conquer mountains and icy landscapes.[1] The capabilities of image manipulation and other editing techniques allow practitioners and artists to fragment nature, display natural processes in non-linear form, and create scenes and events not possible without technological mediations. Our greater access to nature comes about because of technological decontextualization or perhaps *denaturization*?[2] Mediated images of nature are knowable through our cultural codes of understanding, which are shaped by our symbol systems and technologies. We can put nature in the contexts we choose and choose the functions appropriate to those contexts. Nature, in that sense, is a social construct.

PLACE

Place, like nature, is both physical and social. It is a site for and creation of human practice. As geographer Soja (1989) pointed out, space is "both a social product and a shaping force in social life" (p. 7). Places are con-

---

[1] A recent Mt. Everest climbing expedition could be followed each day at www.steponline.com. Nancy Feagin and a crew of climbers reached the summit in late May 2001. Many people, including school children, followed her on the Internet every day of the climb.

[2] The term *denaturization* must be credited to Lance Strate, whose discussions and suggestions were tremendously helpful in developing the manuscript for this book.

structed through the meanings attached to them, discourses surrounding them, and relations operating within them. These form the substance of place identity.

The terms *place* and *space* are sometimes used interchangeably; to clarify distinctions for our purposes, some definitions are in order. *Space* here is a term or principle for organizing thought regarding physical locale or environment. Like time, its conceptual counterpart, *space* is fluid. Critical culture theorists such as Foucault (1980), de Certeau (1984), and Lefebvre (1990) have written about the fluidity of space and the social production of space in everyday practice and power structure maintenance. Foucault and Lefebvre, particularly concerned with economics and power issues, theorized the spatial organization of capital across the globe. They pointed out the relationship between capital distribution and the creation of dominant and subordinate spaces. As Foucault argued, "space is fundamental in any exercise of power" (p. 18). On a smaller scale, de Certeau wrote about how, in everyday practices, people constantly subvert the power hierarchy by literally cutting their own paths through the spatial grids constructed for them. Cultural and postmodern geographers Harvey (1989, 1996) and Soja (1989) are both interested in the use and creation of spaces in late capitalism. They have argued the importance of focusing on the social construction of space and the role of geography in analyses of individual and collective identity. Both contend that space is not a static container through which processes flow, but a construct or entity crucial to the deployment of events in time. Space is a social tradition, a transformation, and an experience.

Place is a specific kind of space—a geographically determined location. Place can refer to concepts like region, nation, or neighborhood or to named sites such as Brooklyn, Baltimore, the American west, or South Africa. These places are rife with meanings created through practices of representation, social organization, and ritual. Place meanings, which unfold in time, are encapsulated in place signifiers such as names, peoples, activities, rituals, built structures, natural characteristics, and social relations. Place, like space (and like nature), cannot be understood separate from human activity and social power relations.

The field of cultural geography focuses on the cultural dimensions of places, including meanings and power relations associated with and operating within them. Many cultural geographers analyze the media and their relationships to place. Duncan and Ley (1993) examined place formation as a function of consumerism within the realm of mass media. Cultural geographers Burgess and Gold (1985), too, examined the ideology of place construction, and particularly the role of the mass media in hegemony maintenance through place representation. Burgess (1990) called for much more geographical analysis of place and nature representations in the media, claiming that the media play a fundamental role in the cultural politics of place and the environment.

The terms *space* and *place* have also been used more frequently in critical media and cultural studies. Grossberg (1992) argued the importance of examining the spatialization of power. He pointed out that it is a bias of modernity that time metaphors are often used in discussions of power. Histories, he said, are also deployed in space. In critical media studies, explorations of place are often related to technologies and power relations. Technologies tend to support or subvert the power structure in shaping places and place meanings. Hay (1993) analyzed the power of the mass media to create perspective on place which "result from, generate and gradually transform relations of power and status" (p. 32). Current media technologies and practices, he argued, have significantly contributed to redefining the spatial features of our environments. He explored specifically how media practices, technologies, and networks have produced a certain sense of territoriality and certain perceptions of space in everyday life. Other media scholars have examined how space is used and created in a number of popular culture and media forms. Zelizer (1992) examined how place is both a physical location and a culturally negotiated term in Israeli radio news. Fiske (1989) analyzed the beach—a construct of popular culture—as a liminal place, partly nature and partly culture. Gumpert and Drucker (1997) wrote about gender and public space, exploring the way gender is both determined by and determining of public space usage.

The places of significance in this book are the midwest region and its larger context, the United States. These two geographic entities, rife with meanings, are characterized in part by their natural environments or the kinds of nature that come to represent them. For example, representations of nature are often used to define regional identities (Fry, 1994; Worster, 1993) and also to define national identity, as many scholars point out (see Crawford, 1992; Daniels, 1991; Pringle, 1991; see also Kinsey, 1989). The American west, as Schama (1995) argued, is signified partly in the symbolic construct *wilderness*, which we imagine to include vast expanses of mountain, desert, and forestland. In the southwest, New Mexico's nature signifiers include desert and cacti, whereas in the midwest, Minnesota's signifiers include lakes and bucolic farmland. Meanings attached to these natural signifiers extend far beyond the natural forms. They speak to ideals. The meaning of the midwest is often tied up with images of agriculture and open prairie land. Nature is coopted to produce imagery and meaning for the region. Likewise, one dimension of the meaning sometimes attached to nature is the context of its placement—of where it is both physically and discursively. Mountains mean something different in the context of the western

United States than they do in Switzerland. The United States and Switzerland are different contexts, and mountains as a physical characteristic of both conjure up different images of each in terms of what they stand for, their history, and how they are used as signs in film, literature, and other cultural forms.

The importance of region and regionalism to nation and national identity, and the specific relationship between the midwest and its nature, are more fully developed in chapter 3. For now, it is essential to examine place and nature in the context of TV.

TELEVISION AND TV NEWS

Television is still the most pervasive electronic medium. Although the Internet and other computerized forms of communication continue to grow in use and garner the interest of a growing number of scholars, educators and advertisers, TV retains its place as the medium most connected to everyday life. Despite an erosion in the time spent with TV due to computers and other media, most households have at least one TV set, as do most dorm rooms, hospital rooms, bars and lounges, physicians waiting rooms, airport terminals, and a host of other private and public spaces. Many of these TV sets are turned on for a good portion of the day. In this respect, TV is almost unavoidable in everyday life. The medium is a physical presence—a source of entertainment, an aesthetic display, and, for many people, the sole source of news and information.

Television is unique in its capacity to represent and create both place and nature. It possesses the technological ability to instantaneously transcend the local and national, and to geographically orient us through its unique perspective. In combination, the network infrastructure; hardware such as cameras, satellites, and computers; videotape and software for graphics and sound; and the production formulas for news programs all work together to represent some of the places, objects, and events that exist and occur in the world as we know it. To put it more strongly, this potent combination in many respects creates those events. They become televisual. This means they are made distinct by the very fact that they are packaged for TV. Nothing is news inherently. Rather, things *become* news on TV and because of TV (Postman & Powers, 1992). The versions or representations of local, national and international events we watch on TV everyday are filtered, focused, decontextualized, and fragmented representations of the places, people and things that exist out there beyond the TV matrix, although in a larger sense, TV imprints all of them. With regard to the 1993 flood, the TV matrix created a unique story about the event and where it took place. Nature and place were key characters.

Television news coverage of the flood was creative camera use and editing, metaphor, and myth all combined in an essentially visual format. The medium of TV, according to Stephens (1998), hungers for short impressions, visual intimacy, fast edits, and what he called *scenes* or *impressions*. Such impressions are synecdoche. That is, they stand for something larger beyond the image. Certainly the TV news stories introduced earlier in the chapter fit the requirements of short impression, fast edits, and scenes. The first story, Mabrey's CBS report from the field, was a montage of impressions about the flood edited together to create a sense of its breadth as well as its impact on the place and its people. In doing so, it created a distinct impression of that area of the country and a distinct relationship between that place and nature. The second montage, the *I Remember* episode, offered scenes from different times and places during the flood period. There was no linear structure to the visuals; they were chosen for their visual and emotional impact.

The entire first story was assembled to create a *where*. It began with the image of the computer-generated globe, then the graphics continued to zero in on a particular place by using maps until viewers visually arrived at a specific place on the globe—the midwestern state of Missouri. The numerous aerial shots from the helicopter that followed the initial maps offered the broadest possible view of the flooded area. Mabrey's use of the war metaphor, as she described the battle against the river, provoked a sense of the river as villain, antagonist, whereas midwesterners were portrayed as protagonist or struggling hero. The other video shots—the farmers, farm equipment, crop fields, American flags, and small towns, which were edited in among the establishing area shots, filled in the impressionistic details of the place and the struggle against evil. Camera angles and shot lengths aided further in creating *scene*. Medium and medium close shots of interview subjects encouraged a sense of the emotional impact. The upward tilt of the camera on sandbaggers encouraged in viewers a sense of their power and determination against the river's onslaught. A downward angle on those wading through the floodwater encouraged a sense of their devastation. The quick pace of the news story greatly enhanced the urgency of the situation. The shots, including the subjects, camera lengths, and angles, combined with the style of editing to create a moving drama of people and place against nature.

The kinds of shots and pacing, and the overall dramatic structure just described, are not unlike those used in many TV news stories. They are prevalent especially in TV disaster news stories. The structure of this story, particularly the use of graphics combined with video images and the reliance on fast edits and images that correspond to reporter narration, is typical for TV news. None of the information, verbal or visual, was unintelligible to viewers who have become accustomed to the format and conventions of TV news generally. As Griffin (1992) argued, the conventions used in TV news lend legitimacy and authority to news stories. The sheer redundancy of format makes it a blueprint for truth or authenticity.

Although news as a media genre—both print and electronic—has been studied and analyzed for decades, the focus has been most often on news as information. Many scholars have focused on the extent to which cognitive information transfer occurs. Some scholars have moved beyond that paradigm to analyze news in other contexts. Of particular note is the work of Bird and Dardenne (1988), who demonstrated that news is often mythological narrative. Zelizer (1992) demonstrated how reporters, acting as a kind of interpretive community, exert enough influence to shape the collective memory of an event. Relatively few scholars have analyzed news visuals specifically, emphasizing not only information content of visuals, but also their function within a news piece.

In his own careful, multilayered analysis of the visuals used in several network news stories within one newscast, Griffin (1992) concluded that TV news visuals rarely serve a purely information function. Rather, he argued, they are more often promotional. That is, most visuals do not add information beyond what the reporter verbalizes. Most often they corroborate verbal information, lend visual authenticity, or provide a transition from one bit of verbal information to another. The stories he analyzed, typical of most daily TV news stories, were filled with file footage, most often the use of which viewers do not question. Such footage acts merely to provide generic, ambiguous scenery, visually proving that, indeed, there was a place where such-and-such happened. We witness such visuals on TV news programs all of the time. Certainly they add nothing valuable to the journalist's scripted story beyond mere illustration. Griffin went on to say that TV visuals are mostly fragmentary. Typically they represent larger, more complex narratives. He used the term *image bites* to describe such visuals. His idea here is not unlike Stephens' notion of *scene*, wherein an impression is made while a larger idea or narrative is nearly conjured up or suggested. The details or full explanation are left outside the frame.

In Mabrey's story and in the CBS *I Remember* episode the visuals were meant to serve a mostly corroborative function; they succeeded in the sense that they offered visual proof of the devastation verbally detailed by each reporter. Yet the visuals did more than that. They added another layer of meaning to the script. The computer-generated maps took viewers on a virtual journey to the flood zone. The use of camera angles and shot lengths encouraged emotional involvement, and the style of editing created a sense of urgency—another, separate visual language. The shot compositions, the fragments of information or image bites, added layers to the verbal details and overall meaning of the story. The choices made to include mostly farmers, zoom in on the American flag, and spend so much time, in the *I Remember* piece specifically, on the crumbling white farmhouse all enhanced the agrarian mythic scope of the news piece. These visuals, woven together as they were in these pieces, created a mythic tapestry of the agrarian midwest, detailing the struggle with nature therein. The visuals of these news pieces, and all of the flood news items before and following them, employed a recognizable grammar of visuals, the rules of which guide not only news visuals, but visuals created for other media, both public and personal. The grammar of visuals, as Altheide (1976) argued, alters reality.

The question to ask, then, is should we concern ourselves with altered reality in a news piece? Is it the responsibility of TV news to replicate reality? Is it possible? The answer to the last question is "no." Television cannot replicate reality. Because TV chooses images and creates visuals in the ways that it does, because of the hardware and software available to package events for TV, it seems reality replication is not really what TV is about. Perhaps a more interesting question is, what *kind* of reality does TV offer? Specifically, what is it about nature and place that we understand from natural disaster news stories on television?

Herbert Zettl, one of the foremost authors of TV production texts and recognized authority on TV aesthetics, detailed the aesthetic requirements of the medium. In an early essay published in 1981, Zettl urged readers not to concentrate continuously on the content of TV, but to focus on the form. He argued that TV should be recognized for what it does best as a medium. Television favors close-ups, it offers a multiplicity of viewpoints, and its main emphasis is on the *now*, not the past or even the future. Television is about the present. To reach its fullest aesthetic potential, Zettl went on, one should make full and good use of a clear set of TV production principles. These include certain ways of using the camera to frame images and certain editing techniques to convey an event in a way that viewers understand and that do not disrupt narrative flow. He detailed specifically in his essay, and in subsequent texts (Zettl, 1990), the correct ways to use two-dimensional space, light, and vectors to create an appropriate illusion of depth and movement. Zettl's ideas extend beyond the merely technical as he has demonstrated, then and now, his understanding of TV's power.

Watching TV news programs, one can often witness careful use of the production principles Zettl advocated. However, in his analysis of more contemporary video—what he called the *new video*—Stephens (1998) argued that TV news is now more apt to transgresses these time-worn principles. According to Stephens, it is becoming more common to see the use of abrupt jump cuts in TV news, and that less emphasis is placed on trying to maintain a sense of visual narrativity by paying attention to continuity of movement in editing. The idea, he says, is to create an impression or scene, or rather a string of impressions, and not necessarily to corroborate an accompanying verbal narrative or description. He explained that such imagery will, in the future, become the norm. Although Stephens considered the emerging visual style of TV and TV news in particular in mostly neutral and sometimes celebratory terms, Cohen (1998) was less enthusiastic. He argued that TV news presents too much visual stimuli; it is too difficult to follow because of excessive movement on the screen. Regardless of one's views about the changing visual style of TV, there is really no going back. Older conventions of TV production are still in use, but are changing as visuals and the technologies used to produce them become more sophisticated and complex.

Although the first story outlined in the chapter, the CBS news piece with Vickie Mabrey, offered a montage of scenes, it more faithfully corroborated her narrative than did the piece from the CBS *I Remember* episode. That episode was filled with strings of impressions, and the overall effect was *scene*. The place and event were more dramatically contrived. Nevertheless, despite differences in visual and verbal style, both pieces faithfully re-created a midwestern mythic identity. In that respect, they were no different from most all of the TV flood news.

2

The Heartland Myth:

Regions, Nation, and Geographic Identity

The pastoral midwest farmlands, lush with corn, soybeans, wheat, and prairie grasses, spread wide and flat to the horizon in some areas, gently dip and roll in others. Solid two-story wood-frame houses with ample porches stand adjacent to prominent barns, filled silos, equipment sheds, and windmills. Architectural configurations such as these stand as islands of habitation amid seas of green growth. Dirt and gravel roads wade through the agrarian waters, leading eventually to small-town oases, the hubs of socioeconomic exchange, and anchors of community and support in these rural parts. One imagines the encounters one might have while traveling within such an area.

You are driving slowly along the quiet, dusty roads, taking time to admire the sky, the earth, the immaculate rows of grain, the abundance. A farmer in seed cap and coveralls rides atop his tractor, moving slowly along the side of the road from one field to another. He volunteers a friendly wave as you carefully pass. When you reach town, you witness, first, a dozen amiable conversations at the coffeehouse. Then out on the street see neighbors greet each other warmly as they go about their daily tasks. Several approach you and, recognizing you as a

35

stranger, offer their assistance during your stay. You discover that the centerpiece of town is the church building, perhaps more than one. Great care is taken to preserve these paeans to God and community, for here people gather to worship, socialize, take comfort, and renew. This place, these people, are midwestern stalwarts. They are strong, accept challenges, and work through their difficulties by drawing on the strength and cooperation of their neighbors. They value hard work, family, God, the land, and their country. Your heart fills as you realize the pervasive sense of safety, security, and continuity here. Soon the sun sets on this landscape of bucolic wonder. You continue your journey. The strings swell, then subside. The image fades to black.

The images presented here are the kinds of images of the rural United States—often the midwest—that we have seen on the large screen and the small, in films and on TV commercials. They are also images created in literature, paintings, photographs, magazines, and other cultural forms. This depiction of the agrarian midwest is not real, but an ideal. Certainly the rural areas of the upper middle states of the United States—often referred to as the *heartland*—are largely farming lands. Many small towns and a number of larger cities are located as commercial, social, and cultural hubs in the midst of agricultural production. In the smaller towns, most people know each other, at least a little bit. Churches, many very old, are plentiful, and a large number of the people who live in these parts do attend weekly services. Yet, although the description of the rural landscape offered here is in some respects accurate, it is only partial. It merely skims the surface of life in the midwest. The idea of bucolic, lush lands, of plentiful crops, family farms, and commitment to land, community, and country appeals to a sense of shared identity. It is foundational to the agrarian myth.

This myth has it roots in the Jeffersonian yeoman farmer ideal and extends into Emerson's 19th century Romantic image of the hardworking, self-sufficient farmer. The myth has held fast in the American imagination. Indeed it serves a vital role in the national identity. The characteristics of the land and the people often conferred on the agrarian midwest are mythic, yet they are necessary for the country to maintain a certain image of itself: hard working, value laden, close to the land, religious. Despite continual social, economic, geographic, and cultural changes, even upheavals, since the beginning of the New Republic, the national identity requires a static set of rural images on which to draw. The family farm is still held as the ultimate icon of Americanness, and the midwest is the geographic repository of that particular vision of the nation. Discourses pertaining to the nation's sense of cohesiveness and shared history call up the vision in many ways and in numerous contexts. The agrarian myth, as demonstrated in this chapter, emerges through various media. It emerged again in fragmented televisual form during news coverage of the midwest flood of 1993.

REGIONALISM

The idea and practice of regionalizing the vast contiguous United States emerged in the latter part of the 19th century. Previously the term section was used to describe different areas of the country. Section implied divisiveness, whereas region implied parts of a larger whole—a notion more socially palatable and politically necessary at that time in the nation's history (Jensen, 1965). Historians, cartographers, artists, politicians, and census takers together developed the practice of regionalizing, although in different ways and for different purposes. Historian Frederick Jackson Turner, famous for his Frontier Thesis, brought the term *region* into widespread use (Limerick, 1987; see also Cartensen, 1965). As the country grew and admitted more states into the union, cartographers, politicians, and census takers used a system of regionalizing the nation as a way to more efficiently handle its size. A given region might be determined by topography, the grouping of states within which it easily fell, or immigration patterns. Artists such as writers, painters, and photographers attempted to capture what they considered the essence of a region—its meaning, history, and landscape—in their creative works. Regions were thought to develop distinctly for the cultural strength of the nation as a whole (see Jensen, 1965). Today regions are identified in many of the same ways they were at the turn of the century, and by many within the same professions, although marketing has increasingly become one of the chief reasons for regional identification and fragmentation. Nevertheless, as time passes and changes occur within the United States, it is interesting to observe the roles and meanings of different regions and the very idea of regionalism.

Although the boundaries of all regions were not then, and are not now, remotely absolute, regions are embedded with meanings or identities. A region takes on meaning through time. Such meanings evolve, yet sometimes remain frozen in a time warp. The meaning of one region, and the reason it takes on that meaning, may be quite different from that of another. Regional meanings are captured, disseminated, and even created in regional imagery. Geographer Bradshaw (1988) discussed the use of regional imagery within literature, the arts, and historical accounts. Bradshaw explained that regional imagery is created in a number of forms and is perpetuated most simplistically in popular culture and mass media. Media images can and often do become stereotypes, and these are difficult to lose. The south as plantations and southern belles; the quaint but provincial northeast; the rude, sophisticated, and hurried eastern corridor; the bucolic yet naive midwest; and the rugged, individualistic west are some examples of over simplifications or regional stereotypes. Regional meanings are encapsulated in signifiers such as land characteristics, people, dialects, architecture, dress, relationships, and so on. When several appear together to create a distinct image, they call up the characteristics of the region. Regional images, although unique to the regions, encourage regional comparison. For example, the image of the old south with its plantations, Confederate flags, and genteel manners implies an industrial, Union north. The simplistic image of the rugged, free-thinking west subtly, or not so subtly, implies its opposite coast with more conventional and often provincial characteristics.

The midwest region, because it has no coastal border, retains a fluidity unique among U.S. regions. It is not dichotomized as are east/west and north/south, and its borders, as well as its meaning, tend to be more malleable. Some states or portions of states are considered midwest in some contexts, but western, eastern, or southern in others. It depends on one's perspective and purpose. The state of Missouri is sometimes the midwest and sometimes the south. Oklahoma changes regions from midwest to south to west. Likewise, Ohio and portions of Pennsylvania are midwestern to some in the eastern states, but definitely eastern to those in other of the middle states. As flexible as its borders are its names. The area more or less considered midwest goes by many, including Great Plains, upper middle states, and heartland, to name a few. For those who wish to make clear not its ambiguity, but its purposelessness from their perspective, the midwest region is called the space between the coasts, flyover country, or the great in-between. It is true that 67% of the American population lives within 1 hour driving time of one of the coasts, and inhabitants of the midwest are aware of their rank on the sophistication ladder as well as the fact that it is conferred by those who do not reside there. However, despite this, most also take pride in many of the characteristics that *are* conferred on them, including wholesomeness, a hard work ethic, and common sense. Because they live within them, residents of the midwest, like all Americans, internalize the regional meanings and simplifications created in the discourses of regionalism. These discourses are components of American national identity and are continually circulated in popular culture forms. We conduct our lives and operate with a basic, although fragmented, understanding of regional myths. One powerful myth is that of the agrarian midwest.

MYTH

Here myth is defined and explored neither as a concrete object nor as a falsehood. Rather it is a form of speech, converted by history and made to seem natural, inevitable. In his much-cited volume *Mythologies*, Barthes (1972) dissected contemporary myths as disseminated in media and other popular forms. He commented specifically on the "natural-ness with which newspapers, art and common sense constantly dress up reality which is determined by history" (p. 11). He referred to the fact that speech forms—and here he included oral, written, and pictorial depictions as speech—are semiological systems, or systems of meaning, that convert history and present contemporary conditions, ideas, or concepts as if they were always that way. They are meant to be as such; they are natural. The very principle of myth, according to Barthes, is that it transforms history into nature. Barthes also called myth depoliticized speech, which means that the process of naturalization defuses language or speech of the concrete struggles—the politics—that brought about the conditions or depictions. Myths, he argued, are not factual systems, but neither are they lies. They are semiological systems. They are distortions. Barthes' ideas about myth are useful when examining regional images and meanings, and when analyzing the mythic scope of U.S. regions.

According to Smith (1985), a single geographic region is rife with meanings circulating in various communication forms. He suggested myth analysis as a way to understand the collective imagination of a society and proceeded to come to such an understanding in his examina-tion of the myth and rhetoric of the American south. Smith analyzed many diverse communication forms—including monuments, literature, corporate reports, addresses, song lyrics, newspaper articles, TV por-trayals, architecture, and the like—and found emerging from them a unified idea or myth, the myth of the Old South. Briefly, the Old South myth encapsulates the idea of the noble Confederacy, where the planta-tion is the centerpiece of drama, and the main struggle is to maintain southern nobility despite forces bent on destroying it. The symbols of the ante-bellum south, vivid and plentiful even today, are enshrined in that region, and elsewhere nationally. They represent the idea of a bro-ken dream. Certainly the Old South myth remains on the national radar screen, most prominently again in the latest battles over flying the Confederate flag over state capital buildings in some southern states (see Jonsson, 2001).

In a similar vein, Limerick (1987) and Slotkin (1992) examined the U.S. west, another deeply mythologized region. Both Limerick and Slotkin focused on the wilderness theme associated with the west, and both argued its importance for the nation in the past as well as today. These historians specifically examined the myth of the frontier, the set of ideas related to western conquest, of land and of natives, as the young nation pushed its boundaries westward. The frontier, or the wilderness, as regionalized in the nation's west is an ideological reference more than a geographic reference, Slotkin argued. Today it symbolizes spiritual regeneration, patriotism, and vigor. Yet the physical west remains an important geographic repository for these national ideals. One need only look at the way politicians use western imagery when they want or need to strongly associate themselves with such ideals. Ronald Reagan did so nearly as a vocation, but Bill Clinton, George W. Bush, and other presidents have also made a point of donning rugged wear and situating themselves at suitable western sites, the more wildernessy the better, for the benefit of news cameras. Photographed images such as these require little interpretation because the meanings are so readily understood and shared.

A common link in the three regional myths outlined here—the Old South, the Frontier West, and the Agrarian Midwest—is the way nature or, more specifically, the land is characterized as an important mythic component. The rugged wilderness, the plantation, and the individual family farm are strong signifiers of regional meaning. They are all three nature in the sense that they contain organic materials, and out of their materials other organic materials can grow and thrive. More important, they are all culture. They are products of history and labor, and they are thick with meaning, struggle, and with politics. War is waging between lumber interests and environmental groups about how to handle hundreds of thousands of acres of western lands (McCarthy, 2001). Farmers have struggled for years with the federal government over farm policies that dictate land use, crop prices, and subsidies. These kinds of struggles are siphoned off when the land is employed to serve as nostalgia or to uphold a region's mythology. As a regional signifier, the land is as indispensable to regional myth as the myths are to national identity.

The geographies of the south, west, and midwest are necessary physical containers, rather conduits, of the mythologies vital to the national imagination. Yet these myths are, as Barthes pointed out, distortions. They are ideals informed by history, yet manipulated for political, aesthetic, or social purposes. The real struggles are taken out—slavery, ousting of natives from their lands—and what remains are romantic, sanitized versions of the past that inform the emotional center of present-day American identity. They become naturalized, simplified, commonsense meanings attached to the regions, and they serve a national function. The means through which regional myths circulate are speech forms, using the term as Barthes did. Yet more broadly, regional meanings circulate via all forms of communications, including mass media and popular culture.

MYTH OF THE AGRARIAN MIDWEST

The geographic midwest maintains responsibility for containing the powerful myth surrounding the family farm and agriculture. The association has long been made between this sort of agrarian life and Democracy. Thomas Jefferson was the first to claim that, "The man who worked the land was upright, reliable, uniquely able to serve his local village and defend his country" (Purdy, 1999, p. 27). Jefferson wrote that farmers were the most virtuous, vigorous, and independent of Americans. They were, he believed, most wedded to their country and the strongest of citizens (Browne et al., 1992). Jefferson's yeoman farmer ideal became even more solidified in the 19th century and most firmly in the literature of Ralph Waldo Emerson. Two themes emerge in Emerson's writings. The first is that nature is a formative element in the American character. The second is that hard, physical labor and self-reliance are prerequisites for achieving the virtues necessary for self-realization (Browne et al., 1992). Emerson believed that farmers lived a morally successful life. Henry David Thoreau, who also contributed heavily to American ideas about life close to the land, believed that the true human purpose was communication with nature. Such ideas have run deep in the nation's sense of self. The land, hard work on the land, and the Protestant work ethic, as sociologist Max Weber detailed in his work, have informed the nation's economy and its democracy (Weber, 1948). Because the midwest region still has a large agricultural economy, it retains the agrarian mythology for the entire country. Yet the images are stuck back in the 19th century. As they argued in their book about the agrarian myth, the midwest and farm policy, *Sacred Cows and Hot Potatoes* (Browne et al., 1992), rural America is seen as the last vestige of the most desirable part of U.S. history. The romantic vision of the country life in the midwest heartland includes a bucolic landscape full of hard-working, middle-class farmers, rolling hills, perfect, neat rows of grain, and pure white homesteads. "This rural America of our dreams persists because it is wrapped up in our desire for ties to the land, economic independence, and community support" (p. 17). The authors continued to explain that this agrarian myth, the most vociferously defended in American culture because it is so desperately desired, has shaped farm policy historically, and ultimately does no service to farmers or agricultural interests.

The term *heartland*, a name often attached to the upper middle states of the nation, is loaded with connotations that reinforce the agrarian myth. Although it is unclear when the term was first used to describe the middle agricultural states, today heartland is used not only to name the region, but also to name thousands of businesses and other interests within the region and even some not within the region.[1] Although the term *heartland* is as abstracted as the region, it conjures up images of trust and simplicity, and when used as the name of a business, evokes soundness and value. In his essay about the heartland, and Kansas in particular, Averille (1999) offered his own definition of *heartland* as "a place where people work hard, lead simple lives and have close ties to the land" (p. 4). However this is only one half of the definition of heartland as it exists in its abstracted form within popular culture, he explained. The other half of the definition is backward mudville, disconnected, naive. Neither is reality, but for some reason the nation needs a dichotomous heartland mythology. The heartland idea exists as a repository of fundamental American values—religion, agriculture, and family. In one term it sums up the whole of the myth of the agrarian midwest.

But true to myth in the Barthesean sense, the agrarian midwest myth is a distortion, a reworking of history into nature. Agriculture is important to this region, but the surface and depth of agriculture is different from that evoked in the mythic imagery. Beyond agriculture there is so much more to the region, past and present. European immigrants to the New World, moving west into the area that is now the midwest, used the land for trapping, hunting, and farming. Along the way, they displaced native tribes who were already there farming and hunting for themselves. Battles, bloodshed, and questionable treaties resulted in eventual European domination of land. Natives not driven from the area were sequestered on reservations (see Levy, 2000). In one historic account of these events, the native tribes of Sioux, Dakota, and Ojibway in what is now the state of Minnesota fought fiercely to keep their ancestral lands. The Minnesota Indian War of 1862 was the pinnacle of their fight against state and federal governments that had broken numerous treaties, forced them into fixed farming areas and methods, and broke other promises they had made to the tribes. A corrupt Office of Indian Affairs in Washington, DC was responsible for the bulk of the misdeeds (Anderson & Woolworth, 1988). The story was similar throughout the upper central region of the newly forming nation. The family farms established by White, European settlers came at the cost of those who had laid claim long before. That emblematic family farm, so cherished

---

[1]Many businesses throughout the United States use *heartland* in their name, sometimes for reasons not completely clear. For example, there is a Heartland Brewery located in the Greenwich Village section of Manhattan in New York City.

by Jefferson and romanticized by Emerson and a host of literary and visual artists since then, was the result of extreme struggle and unfair political maneuvering.

That same emblematic family farm was never as romantic as it was made out to be, and for hundreds of years it has dealt with continuous change and hardship. During the 19th century, farming was undergoing vast changes because of new farming technologies. Farms became more mechanized and specialized. As they grew more specialized, farmers needed to depend more on outside interests; they could not be self-sufficient. By the 1880s, farmers were no longer in control of such things as business cycles, credit, labor supply, price structures, and government policies. Crop transportation was of vital importance to farmers, and lack of railroads in some areas could mean loss of profit. The farmers had no control over the monopolistic railroad system, however. Lack of control, increasing frustration, and financial need caused many to organize and take political action. The Association of Farmers was formed in Minnesota in 1867. The Association lobbied to pass favorable legislation and instituted the coop movement that allowed farmers to buy seed and machinery at lower prices, and to sell for a better profit. Regional alliances similar to the Association grew throughout the region. One result of these Grange politics was the eventual regulation of railroad rates (Saloutos, 1951). Action such as this helped farmers work against sometimes incredible odds. However, between national farm policies and unpredictable weather, farmers have always had to struggle to make a profit. During the latter part of the 20th century that struggle reached its apex in the farm crisis of the 1980s.

Many factors contributed to the mid-1980s farm crisis, but the outcome for thousands of families was the same—a complete loss of land, livestock, and other assets that had been passed down for generations. Farmers with extended credit and not enough income had to finally bail out. Banks sponsored farm auctions almost as a matter of course in many areas. The losses were not just economic. The crisis that hit rural America, and really hit hard the agricultural midwest, was felt emotionally and spiritually as well. Individual farmers, farm families, and farming communities had difficulties coping with the major changes. Depression ran rampant among farmers; many committed suicide. As Dudley (2000) explained in *Debt and Dispossession: Farm Loss in America's Heartland*, distressed farmers tended to suffer alone, veiled in a cloak of silence. The agricultural communities of the midwest tend to foster a stoic sensibility, especially among the male members. The loss of something that has been part of one's family for a long time, indeed that has defined oneself, is difficult to bear and impossible to bear alone. The crisis is not over, and in some areas of the midwest and other rural parts of the country, family farms continue to dwindle, losses continue to rise, as does domestic violence. Depression and suicide remain constant worries.

The fear of what the future may bring sometimes makes farmers and farm families untrusting, and wary of others' motives. There has always been a mixed blessing in being part of a small farming community. On the one hand, you know most everyone and can feel secure in who they are. On the other, you risk constant surveillance, and lack of privacy. Sometimes in small communities change is difficult to accept, and the bearers of change often become recipients of resentment; the outcome is wounds that sometimes never heal.[2] The farm crisis seemed to exacerbate this tendency. As Dudley explained, the pastoral ideal portrait of community that emerged from the crisis was troubling. Under the surface of communal sociability were lingering resentments, unsettled scores, and deep suspicions. Loss of such a magnitude unearthed a multitude of bad feelings. Dudley suggested that the pastoral ideal of unity and cooperation exists in contradiction with market capitalism.

Farmers are business owners. Back in the 1980s, as today, they did not have control over many aspects of their business. In the aftermath of the crisis, finding an easy scapegoat seemed, for some, the logical way to cope. Since the 1980s, the growth of hate groups in the rural midwest has mushroomed (Davidson, 1990). One—the Iowa Society of Educated Citizens (ISEC)—is "dedicated to the proposition that the U.S. is going to hell in a hand basket because of international (Jewish) bankers and their liberal atheistic friends in Washington" (p. 101). Information about such groups and their ideas circulate in newspapers like the National Agricultural Press Association's *Primrose and Cattlemen's Gazette*. Papers like this one include ads for Neo-Nazi groups such as the Aryan Nation, National Alliance, or Christian Identity Movement. Dangerous, reactionary groups are emblematic of some of the worst side effects of job loss within an economy of increasing market concentration. Farming, like all industry, is becoming more corporate, and more concentrated.

Families who did not have to sell their whole farm during the crisis had to sell parts of it or restructure farm management. A number of different labor/management/ownership configurations exist now in the rural midwest. These range from the family farm, which is owned, managed and worked almost completely by one family (the most rare), to the industrial farm which is owned by one group, managed by another, and worked by another (Browne et al., 1992). Corporate farms, which

---

[2]Having grown up in a small midwestern town, the author has seen and experienced first hand the consequences of entrenched ideas and lack of open-mindedness among many small-town residents. Those with innovative ideas or nonconformist actions are often ostracized, leaving them to feel outside the community.

are becoming more common, are one type of industrial farm. The farm crisis brought on this kind of complete restructuring of the rural community, and today the greatest total farm sales are concentrated in the fewest number of farms. In 1995, one quarter of all sales were produced by 1% of farm units (Lasley et al., 1995); today that percentage point is even smaller. Purdy (1999), author of "The New Culture of Rural America," explained that market concentration is found among pork and beef processors as well as in grain farming. "Two companies, Archer Daniels Midland (ADM) and Cargill, are among the top four in all three areas (corn, soybeans and flour) and have been buying up smaller competitors for 20 years" (p. 29). Purdy went on to explain that, as agriculture becomes more expensive and productive, its natural scale is less that of a small farm. The reasons have to do with the advantage of size, the shape of markets, and technology. In 1996, Congress ended price supports and since then huge industrial farms rule the midwest. More families who used to make their entire living on the farm must now rely on off-farm income to make ends meet (Dudley, 2000; Lasley, 1995). A growing class of low-income families resides in the rural midwest.

Many do not stick around. In some counties, there are fewer than two people living per square mile (Purdy, 1999). Small towns that used to support family farm communities are literally closing up shop. Many schools in rural areas, because of low enrollments, have not been able to remain open. Children who live in rural areas must sometimes be bussed great distances to attend school every day. Some live away from home during the week and come home on weekends because they have to go so far (Von Sternberg, 1998). There are those who predict that if the depopulation trend continues, the entire agricultural middle section of the country will eventually become a vast landscape, populated almost entirely by corporate farms, whereas a greater majority of the U.S. population will reside along the coastal perimeters. Those remaining in the agricultural areas who are not farm owner/industrialists will be farm laborers, many of them itinerant, working a number of farms to make ends meet. This is a kind of worse case scenario, but nevertheless the possibility and its implications for the heartland are a far cry from the promise and abundance suggested by the agrarian midwest myth (see Egan, 2001).

CULTURAL FORMS, TECHNOLOGY AND THE AGRARIAN MIDWEST

Mythic agrarian midwest imagery is cultivated through many cultural forms. Indeed these are the very means that ensure its survival.

Especially since the late 18th and into the 19th centuries, literature and artworks such as paintings centered on the agrarian life and experience have led the way in cultivating and circulating regional imagery. Also taking on the task, in an order that reflects technological changes and their corresponding media, are photography, film, radio, TV and, most recently, the Internet. All of them are available today, and all still create, circulate, and challenge midwest mythic imagery. Yet these technologies are not equal in their relationship to the agrarian myth. The differences between print- and electronic-based media are reflected in the ways in which the myth conforms to their specific logics, and to the relationship of the audience to mythic images in these different technological forms.

Chapter 2 included a discussion about the ways in which different media encourage different relationships with nature. We return again to the two strains of thought in media ecology regarding electronic media-dominant culture with respect to nature and place. One strain focuses on McLuhan's argument about the biases of electronic media, whereas the other strain focuses on the revolution of images. Briefly, McLuhan argued that dominant media forms restructure sense ratios and alter one's sense perceptions and experiences of the world vis-à-vis older media forms. McLuhan discussed a return to a mythic sensibility. Such sensibility has been expressed increasingly through imagery, as the discussion of midwest icons and images makes clear.

Before embarking on a discussion of media technologies and midwest mythic imagery, it is important to first outline the variety of media representations of the midwest. Writers, painters, photographers, and filmmakers have all created midwestern images for regional audience members and for audiences that extend far beyond the region. Collaborators in radio and TV have continued that tradition. What follows is a discussion of some of the specific artists and images they have created—some positive, some negative, and some banal—that have influenced the continuity of the agrarian midwest myth. The list is by no means exhaustive, but represents the wealth of images and representations, past and present, circulating in the national discourse. In all of these representations, the midwest stands out as a distinct place within the nation, with a distinct character, and for what seems a national purpose. That character is most often tied to the land and the relationship between land and people.

Ralph Waldo Emerson's writings influenced the idea of farm as icon and farmer as ideal American during the 19th century, and following him were other writers with their own visions of the agrarian midwest. Writing about life in rural Nebraska, Willa Cather (1918), in her novel *My Antonía*, remembered life growing up on the Nebraska prairie. Literary critics have written about *My Antonía* for years, and obviously there is no clear agreement about the novel's meaning or the author's intention (Bloom, 1987). But what the novel represents is life in rural Nebraska at the turn of the 19th century, emphasizing immigrants on the frontier who worked hard to eke out a life there. In his critical essay, Miller (1987) interpreted the novel as a celebration of the prairie—a metaphor for the American Dream. He discussed the narrator's life and other specific images within the novel that lend credence to his thesis. In particular, he focused on an image of a plow on a hilltop, illuminated by the setting sun so that it looms large like a vision, then quickly fades away as the sun disappears below the horizon. Miller interpreted that evocative moment, one of a series of images in the novel that comment on the larger American dream of the promises of the prairie as wilderness and the immigrants who wanted to make their dream come true in that vast open place. It is more a dream than a reality, and it quickly fades away as one realizes lost chances and wasted potential. Regardless of whether Miller's interpretation rings true for other readers, clearly he wrote about this place in the midwest, this landscape, as an important setting on which the American psyche can pin its hopes and aspirations. It takes on mythic importance.

Bill Holm (1985), a native Minnesotan and author of *The Music of Failure* among other works about Minnesota (Holm, 1996), wrote about his relationship with the prairie and the state as a whole. His work celebrates the agrarian life that includes portraying its sad, dark, and lonesome side along with its wholesome, open, and hard-working side. His work is not unlike that of other regional writers, some farmers and other rural folk, who have published work based on their lives (see Wolf, 1995; Hennen, 1997; Hannibal Writer's Club, 1985; Quantic, 1997). Like Cather, Holm's midwest setting is central to the writing. He painted a vivid picture of a place unique in the nation, with a quality of distinction, the subtext of which is a national comparison and perhaps a national longing.

Smiley's (1991) Pulitzer prize-winning novel, *A Thousand Acres*, is the story of a family farm in Iowa, the struggle of survival, and the all-too-frequent isolation one can experience in a remote area as well as the feuding within and between families in this patriarchal order. In her novel, Smiley addresses the quest for more farming acreage as a sign of wealth and a way to one-up your neighbors. The novel poignantly explores the life of this family, mostly through the eyes of a woman, one of three grown daughters of a widowed farmer who lives with her husband in a house next door to him. In true patriarchal fashion, she takes care of her father's every need despite his inability to express love or appreciation. The novel follows the family as it struggles with jealousy, hate, revenge, loss, and change both within the family and within the larger community—a community that tends to alternate between cold detachment and open hostility. The cruel reality of family and social dissolution in Smiley's novel is not unique to this rural area, but representative of the much broader reality surrounding family and social relations. Yet despite its more universal circumstances, the agricultural context remains an important part of her characters' lives and the unfolding plot. The reader is given a wealth of information about farming practices past and present and the work routines and working relationships within a farm family.

Another artist well known for his depictions of Iowa farmland was the painter Grant Wood, who was considered by many a regionalist because of his rural subject matter. Wood and his contemporaries, Thomas Hart Benton and John Steuart Curry, were considered regionalists because much of their work depicted scenes from the central or midwest United States. Woods mostly painted scenes of the agrarian landscape. He is well known for his paintings of farm fields, farm towns, and the inhabitants therein. Some of his best-known paintings are *Stone City, Iowa* (1930), *American Gothic* (1930), *Fall Plowing* (1931), and *Dinner for Threshers* (1934). Some critics at the time considered his works idyllic, whereas others thought it was simplistic. It was well received inside and outside the region, perhaps because it portrayed a life yearned for, an existence that was merely nostalgia by that time, or one that never really existed. Clearly Woods celebrated the farm and rural life, though some of his work revealed critical detachment (Dennis, 1998). John Steuart Curry, considered more socially activist in his work, is well know for *Tornadoes Over Kansas* (1929), *The Mississippi* (1935), and *Boomtown* (1927–1928). Benton's well known midwestern-themed paintings include *Father and Daughter* (1937), *Politics and Agriculture* (1936), and *The Lord is My Shepherd* (1926). This triumvirate of regionalists heavily influenced the whole of midwest imagery within the United States at the time (Dennis, 1998). They remain today well known for their work and their enduring influence on mythic agrarian midwest discourse.

During the same time period, in the early decades of the 20th century, photography—specifically documentary photography—became a powerful and effective means of creating and circulating images of place. Farm Securities Administration (FSA) photographers took some of the most vivid photographs of the midwest of the 1930s and 1940s. The FSA was at first its own department within the federal government, but later the Department of Agriculture absorbed it (Hurley, 1972). FSA photographers, under the direction of Roy Stryker, were charged with traveling through various regions of the United States, at first to record the extent and depth of poverty and hardship as a means to raise national awareness about how people were affected by and coping with the

Depression. Many of the photographs became quite well known, and their images were used over and over again as signifiers of various U.S. regions and the era. Probably the best known of these, taken by Dorothea Lange, depicts a migrant farm woman in California, a mother, staring vacantly into the distance while two of her young children nestle at her neck trying to hid behind their mother. Together the threesome is the picture of destitution. Another photographer, Russell Lee, spent a good deal of his time in the midwest photographing the landscape and the people. A midwesterner himself, Lee had a wonderful rapport with his subjects and managed to capture the essence of rural life in the midwest at that time. His photographs, many of them of poor conditions but not necessarily unhappy people, are in some ways quintessential images of farm life during that period, with emphasis on community, religion, and hard work. Some of his photos, such as *Christmas Dinner in Tenant Farmer's House* that he photographed in Iowa in 1936, look much like Norman Rockwell paintings. Another photo from New Mexico continues his theme of depicting rural community. *At the Community Sing*, taken in 1940, portrays the earnest faces of men from Pie Town, New Mexico, sitting in church, singing hymns with what appears firm conviction. Fixed in time, photos such as these are representative of midwest imagery still fixed in our minds.

Film is the technological successor of photographs. A film, which offers the illusion of motion, is a sequence of still photos, of images that appear in rapid succession and are made to seem alive. As a tool for entertainment, learning, and even propaganda, film has proved a powerful medium of expression. Films can transport someone, as in a dream, for a brief time into another mental state—another dimension. Many fictional and nonfiction films or documentaries alike have used the midwest as a backdrop or central motif for storytelling. In many of these, whether upholding or challenging the idyllic Agrarian myth, the rural midwest retains a mythic aura. The 1989 film, *Field of Dreams*, set in rural Iowa, tells the story of baseball, cornfields, and family, specifically the father–son relationship. It is nostalgic and idyllic, although the main story takes place in the late 20th century. In *Field of Dreams*, filmed in Dyersville, Iowa, the main character and his nuclear family live on a farm in a big, white farmhouse complete with ample porch. He is instructed by a mystical voice to build a baseball field in the midst of his lush, tall cornstalks. He has the unwavering support of his wife and children in his pursuit to somehow reconnect with his dead father by building the field. The cornfield-turned-baseball field as site of father–son reunion in this film offers the audience a chance to reconnect with an American, nostalgic pastoral ideal, baseball and all. Here the family farm becomes, once again, the site for re-establishing a vital part of the national identity.

Mythic midwest imagery circulates in contemporary magazines as well. One devoted specifically to this cause is *Midwest Living*. The bimonthly magazine, a lifestyle-enhancement consumer magazine published in Des Moines, Iowa, by the Meredith Corporation, is clearly geared to the middle and upper middle-income set, which is evident in the ads and features for home decor, food, and travel within the region.[3] The magazine features rural and small-town images in its articles about remodeling projects on farms and in photo spreads of beautiful, green farm fields. Writers wax nostalgic about families, home, and community. Feature stories on the Amish communities of the midwest most clearly illustrate the magazine's preferred vision of the region. In the travel section are listed numerous historic sites such as old farms, Mark Twain's home town of Hannibal, Missouri, or small towns with unique celebrations brought from the Old World. The mythic agrarian midwest lives and breathes on the pages of this magazine.

Radio and TV, completely electronic media forms, continue to extend the mythic agrarian midwest in different formats yet in a similar vein. For over 20 years, Garrison Keillor has hosted his program, *A Prairie Home Companion*, which is produced by Minnesota Public Radio and distributed to a national audience on the Public Radio International network. A featured segment of Keillor's weekly program is his ongoing narrative about the fictional small town of Lake Wobegon in rural Minnesota. Keillor's Lake Wobegon tales, spun out as humorous, touching stories about the people from that town, cover all the bases for idyllic pastoral. Representations woven throughout the tales are the prairie, farms, small towns, and values of community, simplicity, and frugality. Keillor carefully and humorously delineates midwestern insiders and outsiders by religion, ethnicity, and region (Fry, 1998). Television images of the rural midwest have been featured in a number of comic and/or dramatic serials within the past 25 to 30 years. *Little House on the Prairie*, a serial drama series that ran for nine seasons, from 1975 to 1982, was based on the Little House books by author Laura Ingalls Wilder. The show was set in 19th-century rural Minnesota in the fictional town of Walnut Grove, prairie frontier at that time. The heartfelt program focused on the struggles of one family—the warm, hard-working, honest, church-going Ingalls family—that struggled in each weekly episode with the hardships of prairie living, which included those who did not share their closeness and conviction. Because they stood on the moral

---

[3]The most current statistics available for *Midwest Living* magazine readers are from 1991–1993. They indicate that the average household income among the readership is $51,045, that 24% hold professional/managerial positions, and that the highest level of education reached among 55.8% is college plus some years of graduate training.

high ground, nearly every episode ended happily for them, and a lesson was learned by the audience. The backdrop to their struggles was a beautiful, peaceful prairie landscape. It was an idyllic rural setting, reminiscent of the purity and goodness of the land, as reflected in the lives of many of the people who settled there. No mention was made throughout the run of the series of the Native American tribes who had once hunted, farmed, and lived on that prairie before European homesteaders laid claim. The constant villains in the series were the female members of the Oleson family who ran a dry goods store in town (they did not work the land). This family, eastern U.S. transplants, tried hard to retain their eastern sophistication and scoffed on many occasion at the simpler, heartier ways of the other townsfolk and homesteaders, their clientele. The Olesons were often the butt of the jokes and on the wrong end of the moral yardstick in many weekly episodes. Another more recent program set in the small-town midwest was the CBS network program *Picket Fences*, which aired from 1992 to 1996. Set in the fictional town of Rome, Wisconsin, *Picket Fences* was a comic drama series filled with quirky characters and a definite small-town sensibility. This program, too, focused on one nuclear family, the only normal bunch in town, it seemed. The couple—he the sheriff, she the doctor—lived with their three children in a sensible middle-class home. They, too, struggled with issues of right and wrong each week in the context of small town midwestern values, although these were tweaked with characters who were laughably flawed and sometimes hopelessly provincial. The program explored a number of contemporary moral issues, but often from the perspective of trying to open up the minds of these unsophisticated, and trying to work past the small-town problems of gossip and constant surveillance. By Averille's definition, *Picket Fences* represented the negative Hicksville side of the mythic midwest, whereas *Little House on the Prairie* represented the positive wholesome side. Both, as he argued, are simplified abstractions, but no more so than many of the rural midwestern images available on TV.

Many TV commercials employ positive pastoral midwest imagery to sell everything from lemonade to pick-up trucks to insurance and other financial services. The rural midwest, and especially the farm, including farmhouses and crop fields, is used over and over in association with various commodities. Indeed rural images become commodities in themselves, sold again and again to a national audience hungry to consume more of this timeless agrarian past in an effort to retain an important component of their identity as a nation. National identity, too, becomes a commodity. Because we are a nation of consumers, we understand best who we are through the buyer–seller relationship. It makes sense that meanings and identities tied to regional imagery or other specific place images be used to sell products on TV. Television commercial images epitomize the strength and purpose of the medium. They are generally edited in a fast-paced sequence, offering only an impression. Viewers are not meant to dwell, only to quickly consume, and then move on. Commercials are all about the here and now, and only make quick references to other time periods when doing so serves the purpose of creating the right impression for that moment. Quickly we must move on to the next image, the next sale. Commercial images are not unlike images in other TV genres; they are part and parcel of the same medium, the same technology. The electronic medium of TV dominates our media environment, saturating our milieu with its unique logic and perceptual bias. Our acoustic sense is stimulated as we are surrounded simultaneously by image, sound, and movement.

Print media can address the complexities of rural living of the past, present, and future and can delve into the socioeconomic relationships in an area that has relied heavily on agricultural production to generate jobs, wealth, and a social system closely interconnected with a much larger social network—the nation and the globe. Specific media forms that share characteristics with print are painting, photography and film. For example, photography, is a mechanical technology, as is print. Photographs are closely related to books in that both are fixed on paper, representing a static moment in time. Like print, photographs can be mass-produced. McLuhan explained that photographs turn people into things. Of course, he was referring specifically to images of people and how the technology of photography, and later film, turned individuals into icons. Photos of places, too, turn them into objects or things. They are static places within a photo, appearing timeless in their fixity as do landscapes in paintings. Agrarian myth imagery in print-based media encourages a continuous, linear, or sequential experience among readers and viewers.

Television, radio, and computer media, purely electronic forms, emphasize nowness and they demand what McLuhan (1964) called *depth involvement*. Books and other print-based media emphasize linear narrative and visual detachment, not complete involvement. Because of print, we have recorded history. A reliance on print allows us to make reference to the past and speculate about the future. Yet TV takes us out of the linear time–space continuum and brings us into the mosaic of electronic involvement, which has no clear starting point. Although TV requires our depth involvement, it is a paradox in that it does not excite, agitate or arouse, as McLuhan argued. Rather, TV soothes us; it entertains us, to our detriment, as Postman (1985) pointed out in his book, *Amusing Ourselves to Death*.

Television has been described as a mythic force. As a technology and bearer of content, TV distorts, fragments, and reconfigures the realities of the world outside of it. It creates new worlds by connecting distant places and people, and then it tears them apart again in the blink of an electronic eye and with the stroke of an electronic brush. Unrelated sequences of action and unrelated images appear then disappear, gone as quickly as they came. Television and viewers become a community, sharing knowledge and ritual, bonding in the unique space and time of the electronic image infrastructure.

Carey (1988) described TV as a medium of continuity and change. Television brings us together through its rituals of program content and rituals of viewing while changing us through technologies that collapse space and time. Television news viewing, no less a ritual event than drama or sitcom viewing, requires the community of viewers to accept its rules of presentation, its highly stylized, visually stimulating format, and its overall corporate vision of reality. When watching the news, viewers are not typically aware of the layered phases in the process of production or what is sometimes referred to as the *gatekeeping process* (Shoemaker, 1991). The actual labor that goes into each newscast, and the myriad production decisions, are hidden, not meant to be seen, but to appear as part of a seamless entertainment package. Because we must be highly involved with the TV image, it follows that we would necessarily be more involved in TV news than in print news.

The drama of natural disaster news on TV requires an immediate, all-encompassing viewer involvement. The way in which the image mosaic appears on the screen, the variety of focal lengths, and the fast-paced sequence of images demand attention, but of a detached sort. In the case of midwest flood coverage, the familiar icons of the pastoral midwest flitted by, one at a time, in no particular logical sequence. The end result was a gestalt of a place that looked and felt familiar based on the pastoral imagery that came before in other media. The fact that this pastoral landscape was upset increased the immediacy, urgency, and necessity of depth involvement. Viewers paid attention to the fact that the familiar pastoral was somehow askew. That is why it was featured on the news in the first place.

Yet viewers passively took it in, without critical awareness of any broader or deeper implications of this flooding or why it was considered so newsworthy. That is not what TV news asks of us in general. We are asked only to recall the place and note its current chaos. In the case of the flood, viewers were not encouraged to seriously consider why the flooding occurred, why building continued on the natural flood plain, why economically disadvantaged groups were harder hit, or what it meant in the past and means now to have altered the course and flow of the Mississippi River with a complex series of locks and dams over hundreds of miles of its flow. Although some on-camera reporters and studio newsreaders did address the issues of building in the flood zone, controlling the river's flow, and continual federal relief for flood victims, the images discouraged any real consideration of these issues. The sheer movement of images in flood-related newscasts was mesmerizing. One could be caught up in the intensity of the emergency. Who is victimized? How severely? How are they coping? What are the immediate dangers? Just as quickly as the images appeared, they were gone. After about 2 minutes, the newscast had moved onto the next disaster or next image-driven political scenario. Perhaps an automobile commercial interrupted the newscast, complete with its own set of rural or wilderness imagery. Tough trucks roared through the wilderness, defeating mountain peaks on their way to the plateau. These machines are meant to control nature completely. The jarring contrast between the disaster news images and commercial images was lost on most viewers. Nature was being used to serve different televisual purposes in each context. That they appeared together in the span of a few minutes on the same screen is part of the mosaic of TV. One literate in the contrasting, non-sequential imagery of television allows the images and any larger implications to wash over them. Viewers continuously expect to be hit with the next big wave. No one need become absorbed in the place, come to be involved in it the way one does when reading a novel or when viewing a still painting or photograph. In those cases, one's eyes are fixed and one's orientation is controlled, slowed down, absorbed, sequential. One ponders and is not merely overwhelmed for a fleeting moment.

HEARTLAND CONSTRUCTION IN NETWORK FLOOD STORIES

Heartland imagery pervaded the flood stories on TV, particularly on the networks. Sometimes its was subtle, merely a suggestion; other times it was a bold statement. Following are descriptions and analyses of network flood stories typical of the coverage appearing all summer long on ABC, CBS, and NBC evening newscasts.

On July 7th, still early in the flood, *ABC's Nightline* with Ted Koppel was devoted to the midwest flood. The agrarian midwest was mythically characterized as the land of stalwarts in this 1-hour presentation. Koppel, seated in his New York studio, introduced the flood story at the top of the hour. Then he introduced Dave Maresh in the studio who, seated next to Koppel, reported on rainfall levels in the midwest and levee heights along the rivers. Viewers looked at computer graphic maps of the area and graphic illustrations demonstrating rainfall measurements and levee constructions as Maresh spoke. Next, reporter

Chris Bury, a correspondent in the midwest, added a dramatic flourish to Maresh's straightforward chant on levees and rainfall statistics. After a series of shots from inside one Army Corps of Engineers station— filled with computers and lots more sophisticated electronic equip- ment—Bury exclaimed in voiceover that, "The battle stations were bustling today at the Army Corps of Engineers command center in Rock Island, Illinois, but the army appears to be losing this war." His use of the war metaphor here is particularly apt because of the Army Corps angle. Bury went on to describe the power of the Mississippi River. "The Mighty Mississippi is spilling over its banks," he said; as he spoke, a Corps engineer spokesperson appeared on screen riding in a helicopter. The engineer, Dale Rossmiller, spoke briefly about the flooding in the area, then cautioned that, "The efforts of man in a flood like this seem miniscule compared to the power of the river." Bury finished his seg- ment of the report by saying that, because more rainfall is predicted, the Army is all but helpless.

Having established for viewers that the river, a mighty force, was fighting the people, the program continued with a shot of Koppel, in New York, who prepared the audience for an interview with two of the flood victims, both from Davenport, Iowa. On split screen, the audi- ence could watch both interview parties. Koppel, in medium shot, was seated in his studio on screen left. On screen right stood the two Davenport residents on location. They were presented in both long and medium shot at night, standing stiffly on the edge of the flooded river. One interviewee was Helen Swisher, a 60-something woman, the other was Tim Cavanaugh, a 30-something man, manager of a riverfront restaurant in Davenport. Koppel spoke with Cavanaugh first about his business and how the flood had affected it. Then Koppel addressed Swisher. She was upbeat about the flood, explaining that, although the flood has interrupted her life and the lives of her family members, she is trying to enjoy it. "The children are just having a ball," she said. "We fish, play cards, and we're just trying to enjoy." She explained how won- derful her family has been and how wonderful the firemen and police- men had been throughout all of the flooding. She appeared nonplussed as she described sitting back and watching various pieces of furniture float by her house. When Koppel commented on her spirit, she explained, "Our whole family's like that. We try to make the best of everything, and hope that something good will come out if it."

Next, Koppel addressed Cavanaugh again, asking about cooper- ation in the city during the flood. Cavanaugh described how everyone in the city has pulled together since the flooding. "They've all tried to pro- tect each other and help each other. It's amazing how the populace has pulled together. It's an attitude of the city to help each other, and keep each other together as much as possible," he explained.

Koppel concluded the interview by telling them, "You're both an inspiration, you really are." Back in full screen, Koppel, speaking directly to the TV audience right before the commercial break, said, "When we come back we'll be joined by a frontline fighter in the battle against the floods." On return to the program, Colonel Albert Kraus, in Rock Island, Illinois—right across the river from Davenport—appeared on screen in medium shot. Standing in front of a wall map in an Army Corps of Engineers office, Kraus described the fighting techniques being used against floodwaters. "We continue to work with many others," he explained as he described fighting techniques, including technical expertise, sandbags and flashboards. Continuing with the war metaphor, he went on, ". . . fighting to the point where mother nature overrides us. If we're losing battles, it's not because of lack of spirit." He concluded by saying he has nothing but praise for the people in the region because of their hard work and cooperation. Following Colonel Kraus' expert assessment of the situation, Koppel returned to full screen, described the topic of tomorrow's program, and signed off for the evening.

In typical *Nightline* format, Koppel held reign in his studio while reporters joined in, both in the studio and from the field, aiding Koppel with supplemental material relevant to the evening's topic. This evening it was the same. Koppel controlled the pace and direction of the flood program, while reporters Maresh and Bury, aids to the news monarch, played supporting roles, offering background information, traveling to this remote place, gathering images, and orchestrating interviews for Koppel's ease and convenience. Without having to leave his news throne, Koppel could address his midwestern subjects. His voice and image were a familiar, authoritative presence on the screen, speaking from the center of news and the center of power in general: Washington, DC. Those he interviewed from the midwest were the victims fighting a good fight and maintaining hope. All three interviewees—Swisher, Cavanaugh, and Kraus—epitomized the hard-working, stoic, and community-minded midwesterner. It is uncertain how the interview subjects were chosen for these *Nightline* segments, so it is impossible to determine what producers, reporters, and Koppel, were looking for specifically. It is clear, however, that what they got were three people who presented a bold face to the TV screen, upholding the typical midwestern image of a sound work ethic, sensibility, and good humor.

In contrast to the spirited and hopeful interviewees in this *Nightline* episode were many other midwesterners, in Davenport and other cities deeply affected by the flood. A large number were forced by police and Army National Guardsman to leave their homes. Many resisted because they had no place else to go and they disagreed with authorities about the extent of the flooding and its potential threat. An examination of local flood footage from WHBF-TV, a CBS affiliate in

Rock Island, Illinois, reveals quite a bit more coverage of the human-scale problems caused by the flood, especially in working-class and poor neighborhoods—those built in low-lying areas close to the river. The Garden edition, a neighborhood in Davenport, was especially hard hit. Local news stories from this area included images of police in verbal bouts with visibly anguished residents. Davenport mayor Pat Gibbs also appeared, urging residents to leave. These people were not putting on a stoic face for the camera. They were upset, afraid, and showing their fears about not having control over the fate of their homes. The reporter interpreted, saying, "some people think city officials are most concerned with looters, not lives." One neighborhood resident, a woman, interviewed for the segment said that, "These people have lived here all their lives. Why would they take something from each other?" Another local segment from KSDK in St. Louis reported on July 12th about the local River des Peres area evacuation. There were many shots of mobile homes in that section of the city. There were also shots of upset residents. Some people interviewed on tape verbally expressed their outrage. The report included information about how electricity was cut off and moving companies were engaging in price gouging. Although local news stations were more apt to include these sorts of images and information from flood-ravaged areas, few network stories did. The *Nightline* episode from July 7 was an example of how midwesterners were typically portrayed on network news in general.

On July 21, *Nightline* did it again. In one segment of this second program dedicated to the flood in its later stage, they followed one retired woman, Lois McDonald, with a camera as she surveyed in disbelief the flooded area around her home, and then sought help in a makeshift office space set up just for people in the area who were seeking federal flood relief. Reporter Mike von Fremd, who compiled this story, said in voiceover during the segment that McDonald "Prides herself on being a tough midwesterner." To corroborate that characterization, McDonald explained on camera that "Iowans are tough people." The nation of viewers could rest assured. Despite the awful conditions many found in their living quarters, they would not be defeated in spirit. Locally, things might look different, but from the networks' eye view, strength of spirit had to remain constant.

That same sense of strength, coupled with the image of the family farm and the individual farmer, was pervasive throughout the summer's network flood coverage. On July 31, NBC's Kenley Jones, in a 1-minute, 40 second segment of that evening's news, focused exclusively on how the flooding had affected two family farms. Specifically, he recounted the fate of two individual male farmers. The first shot on the TV screen was a long shot of two farmers, each holding onto a single wooden stake while one of them hammered it into the ground. The stake was marked in inches to measure the depth of flooding. The two men stood next to a crop field that had begun to fill with water. Jones explained in voiceover that the two men were farmers, Leroy Soudeth and his son, who own a farm together in Missouri close to the flooding Missouri River. Then he explained that the image just seen was footage taken several weeks ago before the flooding had completely taken over the field as well as the farm buildings. As he mentioned this, viewers saw moving helicopter shots of the entire farm to date, soaked beyond recognition. Jones went on to say that Soudeth and his son had lost the year's corn and soybean crops. In the next shot, Jones appeared on screen, in medium shot, inside the helicopter. He was trying to speak above the whirring helicopter blades; his hair was blowing across his face. On the left screen, behind and below Jones, was a clear shot of flooded rural Missouri. Jones announced that they (he and the news crew) could not find Leroy today.

The next shot in this story is also from an earlier part of the summer—3 weeks earlier Jones explains. The shot is a long shot of Jones in conversation with a different farmer, Dale Hahn, of Foley, Missouri. The camera, situated in front of the two men, moved with them as they walked toward it through Hahn's field, absorbed in conversation. Jones' voiceover described Hahn's 600-acre farm. Immediately following that shot was a shot of the same field, as of July 31, completely flooded. In

Farmer in the field

this shot, Jones and the farmer were no longer walking through the field. Rather they were riding through it in a small motor boat. Cut to a close shot of the farmer's face as he maneuvered the boat through what was once a field of corn. Next, viewers saw a quickly edited sequence of shots of the farm, farm buildings, and the house he rented out to a tenant farmer (as Jones explained in the voiceover). Then in medium close shot, Hahn said matter of factly, "I've lost a whole year's income." Jones filled in the details by explaining, over the next few shots, that the income he had lost was about $90,000, and none of it insured. The next shots were all of the farmer. First he appeared in medium shot, then in close shot in front of the house we had seen earlier. Next came another shot of him in the boat as the camera slowly moved closer to his face. Over this final image, Jones finished the segment by saying, "The great flood of '93 has broken all records."

Putting an individual face on a news story of magnitude, no matter how great, is something TV news does particularly well because TV cameras can visually portray individualized, concrete social problems particularly if they are visually dramatic. The flood as a visual drama was an immediate problem for people directly affected and much easier to portray than poverty or the health care crisis, for example. However, the flooding was large in geographic scope and material loss, and it implied a long history of river control and building on the flood plain, all of which was difficult, if not impossible to portray visually, especially on the small screen. Individualizing the loss was a way to create a personal context for such an overwhelmingly large phenomenon. Zettl (1981) argued that the talking head on the small screen is ideal for TV. What distinguished so many of the network flood stories was the type of individual chosen as the face of this disaster. Often it was an individual farmer, mostly it was male. He was typically shot in one of his crop fields, either standing alone or walking with a reporter. These specific shots were included 32 times in network flood coverage alone. The farmer was chosen as the representative of the idea of the midwest. He epitomized the ideal midwesterner—stoic in character, strong, of few words, and clearly hard working, as evidenced in his rough, lined face and the seed cap he inevitably wore to shield his head from the outdoor elements. The yeoman farmer, the individual representing the family farm, the commonsense, rooted, hard-working man celebrated by Jefferson and Emerson, was alive and well in TV flood news. Occasionally he was accompanied outdoors by wife and children, but mostly he was alone, facing the loss himself, explaining only a little, disguising a lot.

The use of medium close and close shots on individual faces, as in the prior story, is a camera technique and visual code that encourages

Farmer's face

viewer identification and emotional attachment. Often in a TV disaster story, viewers see close shots of people who have suffered loss. In voyeuristic fashion, viewers are given the closest possible look at the anguish experienced by those who have suffered shock or loss of some sort. Yet the close shot is also used as an attempt to generate emotion. Because many of the farmers who appeared in flood news stories showed little emotion on camera, news crews tried to compensate by adding emotion in the way of shot length variety and in editing together medium close shots with close shots or moving in on a subject's face, as the camera did on farmer Hahn in the NBC story. In contrast to the close shots on interview subjects, reporters almost always appear in medium or medium long shot—a code for authority or detachment. Occasionally the camera moves in for a medium close shot on a reporter, but never a close shot. Those are reserved for the victims. The victims in this case were the farmers; their material losses were the nation's emotional losses. Television cameras and news crews did their best to pinpoint, and even create the sum of this loss.

The use of the war metaphor, employed over and over again in all TV coverage of the flood, strengthened the sense of the farmers' victim status and directed blame for their losses and the losses of everyone else along the flood route. In network coverage, the war metaphor was used verbally 32 times. The networks typically focused on the flood—on mother nature—as the source of all this loss. There seemed no other explanation. In fact, the losses incurred during the flood had a lot to do with the fact that a certain amount of flat land adjacent to a river, natural flood plains especially along the major arteries in the middle of the country, have filled regularly to accommodate river overflow during periods of heavy rainfall, sometimes yearly. Some cities in the midwest and elsewhere have conceded the need to allow a certain amount of land to remain flood plain and have stopped building on that land (Charlier, 2000). As historian Steinberg (2000) argued in his book *Acts of God,* many natural disasters, and certainly the flood of 1993, are not completely mother nature's fault. Steinberg pointed, rather, to human fault. People have allowed building and farming to continue in areas that are prone to disasters such as flooding rivers. A number of developers have continuously tried to turn a profit on suspect real estate. Steinberg offered the example of St. Charles County in Missouri, located at the confluence of the Mississippi and Missouri Rivers, where low-income housing has repeatedly been built on low-lying lands close to the two rivers. Government bail-outs and levees built to protect, however spuriously, these housing areas have encouraged builders to continue making a profit on real estate sales and rentals in an area meant to act as a flood plain. Government agencies, farmers, and other business people have also continuously worked to control the flow of the rivers through locks and dams and higher and higher levee systems, narrowing the river and forcing a faster flow. McPhee (1989) wrote a detailed account of government intervention on the Mississippi River, focusing on the Army Corps of Engineers in particular. A list of farming techniques that encourage excessive flooding on the flood plain include draining previous wetlands for crops (Grunwald, 2001; Millett, 2001). Such acts of "man" keep the rivers from following their original course and maintaining their natural level. The resulting human losses deny the fact that river flooding is a normal occurrence. As argued in chapter 2, a disaster is defined when human losses have occurred. The disastrous flood of 1993 in the midwest, clearly the heaviest flooding the midwest had experienced in a long time, was difficult for many to endure, and the losses—of homes, businesses, and even a few loved ones—was a sad phenomenon. Yet it was also an example of how nature was not entirely to blame.

Yet blaming nature was the overwhelming context and overriding argument in the majority of TV news stories. The midwesterner as victim, the farmer as victim, offered an easy and dramatic explanation. The worn, hard-working, and hopeful faces of the farmers and other midwesterners briefly garnered the attention, pity, and admiration of the nation's viewers. The networks fed them a heavy diet of heartland images that upheld mythical notions of that place, those people, who represent the best of who we as a nation like to believe we are.

In addition to portraying the stoic character of the midwestern-er, particularly the midwestern farmer, network news stories also included images that corroborated the religious and patriotic aspects of the agrarian midwest. Many network stories, especially at the height of flooding during the month of July, included helicopter shots of flooded small towns, where mostly only rooftops were still clearly visible. In these moving shots, panning the length of town, the camera would often capture a church steeple, tall and pointed skyward, standing proudly as flood waters surrounded it. The church steeple was a marker of hope, perhaps, that the loftiest ideals of the community would remain untouched. Sometimes the sky camera would linger on the steeple. Other times it gave the steeple a prominent space within the panning shot, indicating that the church building was the center of town. Images of churches and references to religion and churches occurred 25 times in network coverage.

ABC's report of July 27 included a segment from Erin Hayes in the small town of Grafton, Illinois. Both on camera and off, Hayes described the struggles of the small town and the damages to the water treatment plant, fire department, and police department. As she described the town's troubles, viewers watched an edited sequence of shots of buildings in town, sandbagging, and people moving out. In the middle of the report, a camera set up in a moving boat lingered on a medium long shot of a church with a tall steeple on screen left, with another square building on the right. The image remained on screen much longer than the other images in her report. Finally, as she finished, she explained that the people of Grafton ". . . . pray they can keep it all going when the water is gone." On July 29, ABC's Erin Hayes reported again on the extent of the flood to date. This report, from Alton, Illinois, is filled with allusions to the power of the river, accusing it at one point of "shoving, stretching and snatching things." The 2-minute, 30-second segment from Alton ends with an image of a white church with a tall steeple standing in several feet of flood water. Immediately before this shot, Hayes, in voiceover, is talking about what the residents of this small town hope for in the near future. Accompanying the final church image, a long shot slightly from below, are her words, ". . . . that is the prayer here." The message was clear in these reports: The church is a central building, and religion is a central support for the faithful mid-westerners struggling to make sense of a long and arduous flood.

Sometimes the image of the church steeple appeared in news reports that also included images of the American flag. The two seemed to go well together, as demonstrated in the following ABC, CBS, and PBS July reports. In its July 22 report, ABC news opened the story with an image of a church steeple sticking out of the floodwaters engulfing

Church shot

the historic town of St. Genevieve. Later in the report, the mayor of the town is interviewed in front of what appears to be a civic building. In medium close shot, the American flag is clearly situated to the mayor's left as he explains the city's struggles and hard work. On August 2, CBS began its report from rural Illinois. The first image on the screen was from a helicopter panning the length of a small town, then lingering on the church steeple as reporter Vickie Mabrey, in voiceover, finished her introduction of the site of the day's flood news, the "small farming town of Valmeyer, Illinois." Mabrey's report closed with the camera lingering on an image of an American flag sticking out of the water somewhere in Valmeyer. The flag image appeared 58 times in network flood coverage.

Religion and patriotism—twin ideals—were prominently displayed through the images of church and flag, although with hardly a verbal mention of religion and none of patriotism. Yet the images spoke loud and clear. In them alleged religious and patriotic fervor were offered up as pillars of midwestern strength. Perhaps it was more of a national yearning or, more strongly, a nationally shared belief. In *Blood Sacrifice and the Nation*, scholars Marvin and Ingle (1999) discussed the religion of patriotism in the United States. The powerful presence of the flag, displayed prominently and abundantly in the mass media, is a totem of this civic belief, they argued, and keeps the totem systems "vibrant, effective and ever-present " (p. 6). The presence of the flag over and over in flood news stories signaled the nation's patriotic religion as well as its unity in sacrifice—a necessary sacrifice in the fight against

Flag shot

deadly nature. The images of church and flag, representing twin religions, offered not only strength and a sense of hope, but also a sense of irony to the news reports. Despite their beliefs, in God and country, midwesterners were dealt a blow by severe forces. They were not being spared. Yet optimism ran high, at least the way network news constructed it. It is no surprise that the use of the war metaphor was so prominent, as were references—sometimes in word, but mostly in image—to forces to aid in the battle: both church and state. Supplications to God and pleas to the federal government for aid threaded throughout the network reports, particularly during the worst moments in the month of July. What followed during the summer were news reports of more destruction and lots of the aftermath.

The agrarian midwest myth and it concomitant images—diffuse yet constant—peppered network news stories during the tenure of flood coverage. Television offered a continuous, yet fragmented heartland. The story of the flood was an interrupted narrative. Yet interruption is inherent to TV, especially TV news. The news format, coupled with a constant flow of commercial messages, results in a program that is little more than bits and blips edited together. It is a mosaic of information without solid form, yet reminiscent enough and referencing all of the words and images of the the representations of the midwest that have come before in other media and in other times. They were retained in the national collective memory and played back during the summer of 1993.

3

Landscapes of Disaster:
Visual Aesthetics of Flood News

In early August 1993, a flood-defining moment occurred. It offered the networks, some of the local stations, and many postflood documentary producers an outstanding dramatic image that could be used over and over again as a way to illustrate damage, destruction, and river rage in the heartland. On Sunday morning, August 1, the Columbia levee on the Mississippi River near Columbia, Illinois, gave way. Television news crews, which had been on alert for days because they knew the break was inevitable, captured from the safety of overhead helicopters the moment of the break. Viewers locally and nationally witnessed the tumultuous water rushing through. What happened next made for some of the most memorable and most referenced flood footage. The rush of water quickly demolished a farm located within yards of the levee. Network and local cameras captured the scene in which a three-story white farmhouse, silos, equipment shed, and other buildings were literally crushed and swept away. The farmhouse, however, was the focal point of the shots in most of the footage aired live and in later broadcasts. Cameras followed the water's movement every second: from the initial rush through the broken levees, its approach toward the farmhouse, its literal dismantling of the house, and finally its washing the pieces away with the renegade flow. There was really no need to manipulate the image with camera tilts, edits, or zooms in or out. All of the energy was right there in the subject.

Despite a similar focus on the farmhouse structure, different news stations chose slightly different ways to present the image during their news programs. Necessarily, each captured the event from a different camera angle,[1] and each made its own voiceover choice. Two of the networks chose to underscore the powerful image with their own color commentary—words attesting to the river's power and implying the people's lack of same. ABC's Richard Gizbert announced over the unfolding image that "The Mississippi was claiming more territory, more victims early this morning, gushing over a levee in Columbia, Illinois. People were evacuated from water that swept aside a farm and toppled silos like bowling pins, and trees like twigs." NBC's John Gibson remarked over the images that, "The swollen Mississippi River clearly demonstrated its power today. Breaching the levee at Columbia, Illinois, flood waters lifted and shattered a farmhouse in a matter of minutes." CBS's Sandra Hughes opted to remain silent as the footage aired. Perhaps she recognized that no words were necessary. Local stations in St. Louis televised the levee breach live at 9:15 a.m. They had no time to decide how they would present the image; it unfolded before them and their viewers simultaneously. KSDK, the local NBC affiliate, featured reporters in the helicopter and in the studio taking turns exclaiming about what they were watching as the farm buildings were demolished in the rush of water. The KSDK helicopter reporters noted, and viewers could see, that the equipment shed went first, but the camera really focused on the farmhouse, following each second of its demise until it was merely a bunch of wood scrap bobbing and weaving, then disappearing, in the dirty flood water. KTVI, the ABC affiliate at the time, also captured and aired the scene live. Although their camera followed all of the farm dismantling, it did not train specifically on the house. The shot was a much longer shot and included all of the farm buildings at once. The reporter in the studio remarked right after that "Grain silos crumpled like a rotted piece of tin foil." The local stations, although working without a script, were clearly as awed by what they were witnessing as were the networks.

---

[1]Because of the many different angles at which the farmhouse destruction was captured from the sky, it seems there must have been news helicopters swarming the area. According to Pete Barrett, News Director of KMOV-TV in St. Louis, the helicopters were everywhere in the sky in that area for 2 to 3 weeks, and the local helicopter company made a substantial profit by leasing both to local stations and visiting network crews.

The farm dismantling footage provided the kind of visual feast for which TV crews yearn. The dramatic, awesome shot was the quintessential midwest disaster landscape. It captured the river, thought to have been controlled, destroying a timeless and beloved sign of agrarianism. This brief footage also signaled a turning point in flood news coverage because it encapsulated the battle between humans and nature, which had, by early August, definitely turned in nature's favor. The white farmhouse, icon of the mythic agrarian landscape—helpless in the river's onslaught—was beautifully captured on videotape. From that day on, this shot, at whichever angle each camera had captured it, became the most widely referenced shot in later flood news on all three networks and in a number of documentaries made about the flood. After August 1, when flood news coverage was no longer a nightly feature on network news, the farmhouse shot was shown 72 times on the three networks until virtually the end of regular coverage in early 1994. The shot was used in local and national postflood special documentaries as well. KTVI and KSDK both featured the farm dismantling in their flood news compilation documentaries. The KSDK flood special featured the August 1 footage at the beginning of the documentary as part of an introductory image montage. The live coverage aired August 1 was included later in the tape. KTVI did not include the farm dismantling shot at the beginning of its compilation documentary, but did include it

Farmhouse shot (August 1)

in three different places later within the documentary. In 1995, *Nova*, the PBS syndicated program, aired a special documentary entitled *Flood*. *Nova*'s documentary opened with an image of another sunken white farmhouse, not the one previously described, but one hit on that same day in that same area. Later in the program the famous August 1 farmhouse shot was given ample air time. The *Nova* special identified that the farm belonged to Virgil Gummersheimer; included was a few seconds' interview with Virgil and his wife (not identified by name) immediately after the dramatic footage of their collapsed farmstead. The farm footage was used again at the end of the special. Finally, the CBS *I Remember* flood retrospective featured the August 1 shot three times—once in the introductory image montage, then at several angles in the middle of the piece, and once more at the end.

The August 1 farmhouse destruction, emblematic of the agrarian myth, became a televisual metaphor for this televisual epic. The family farm was dismantled before the camera and inserted countless times in ensuing flood coverage. The image was used both aesthetically and ideologically. These few moments of chaos captured on tape and inserted regularly into the nightly news and on documentary features symbolized the height of chaos wrought by nature's destruction on the heartland. Coverage thereafter, particularly on network nightly news, focused visually on repairing the heartland, and particularly the farm—an ideal heartland landscape. During later daily coverage on the local and especially network news, as the rivers slowly receded, camera-created landscapes of the flood's aftermath often were juxtaposed visually with shots of the earlier, more chaotic flood period and frequently without any clear indication to viewers about when the August 1 farmhouse footage or other shots of flood chaos had been taken, or how they related to what was shown at the moment. Although such time manipulation via file footage is a common news practice (see Epstein, 1973), especially when covering long-term events, focusing on time and information manipulation through visuals on TV news forces one to question the extent of event construction as opposed to mere event reporting, as journalism claims to do. In the case of televised journalistic coverage of the flood, time manipulation of this sort underscored the fact that TV was creating an epic—one that unfolded in mythic, televisual time.

Natural disasters in general are dream stories for TV news. They deliver some of the best possible visuals to cameras and audience members hungry for drama. News visuals inform in ways different from words, and TV as a medium of communication presents visuals differently than does print (Graber, 1990). Although viewers take in the visual, aural, and textual elements of TV news all at once because they are intertwined and often simultaneous, this chapter focuses exclusively on visuals—specifically, camera shots, computer-generated maps and graphic still store images used mostly on network daily coverage and in postflood documentary coverage. Television cameras framed, and graphic icons and maps identified, nature and the midwest in a way that conformed to shared aesthetic and mythic ideals. Yet TV created an epic all its own. Television cameras positioned a nation of viewers as tourists to the area—outsiders—by fixing their gaze above and geographically beyond the disaster, yet offered them an immediate experience of it by framing landscapes of disaster that reinforced, re-created, and altered conceptions of nature and the midwest. Ultimately, TV, in its capacity to uniquely manipulate time and space, created its own mythic heartland.

LANDSCAPES AND NATURE

The term *landscape* has been used in a variety of ways to denote various spatial contexts. Within the social sciences, sociologist Zukin (1991) and Geographer Harvey (1989) examined urban and global landscapes as repositories of economic organization. Literary critics have used the term *literary landscape* to describe settings created and/or represented by novelists. For example, Rundstrom (1995) analyzed Willa Cather's interpretation of the prairie landscape in *O Pioneers!*, and Saglia (1996) explored the distinctive features of literary landscapes in 18th-century Gothic novels. A number of art historians have traced the history of landscape painting within the 18th- and 19th-century Euro-American traditions (see Fuller, 1985). Geographers Cosgrove and Daniels (1988) focus on how the natural order of the earth and the types of relationships humans have with it—and each other—are represented in 18th-century landscape painting. These authors pointed out the significant mystifying effect such portraits have in that they provide the illusion of order while reifying domination: of people over nature and landowner over laborer. In all of these analyses, landscape is both a context for and creation of human activity.

Here, too, landscapes are defined as cultural creations and contexts. Drawing insights from historian Schama (1995) and geographers Larsen (1992) and Daniels (1991), the argument is made that landscapes are cultural creations that employ a variety of media and technologies and use the natural world as subject matter. Landscapes define a natural order that is in essence a social order. The choice of subject matter, the composition, and the framing of a landscape speak volumes about our aesthetic traditions, the ways we think about and have access to nature, and how we have come to gaze upon it. They also speak to human relationships with nature and with each other.

Natural landscapes are often associated with terms such as *picturesque, pastoral, rural,* and *wilderness.* Each of these terms connotes nature from a human perspective, and each suggests a degree of human interaction. For example, the wilderness landscape, although we consider it that which is least marred by humanity, is our own creation, "borne of culture's craving" (Schama, 1995, p. 7). Schama pointed out that all landscapes are the work of the collective mind, and wilderness is as much a product of culture as any other landscape. Contemporary wilderness landscapes are framed within national parks; at designated scenic overlooks along roads and highways in remote areas; within religious tradition; in media such as paintings, photographs, and literature; and, of course, on TV. Landscapes are the work of the collective mind as shaped by culture, including technology.

Literary landscapes and landscape oil portraits are products of print-based culture; they reinforce a perspective on nature as removed, objectified, and controllable. The invention of the camera allowed new ways to create and reproduce landscape images—first in photography and later on film and videotape. Now, in electronic media-based culture, via TV and the Internet, we enjoy different kinds of images of nature and the environment, and we can produce and experience different kinds of landscapes. Electronic technology often presents landscapes in discontinuous, fragmented fashion, and viewers are required to piece them together to provide closure. Because the small screen cannot adequately offer broad landscape vistas, the camera frames pieces at a time. Sometimes they appear in sequence, and sometimes they are juxtaposed with shots of other objects, other action. The camera will often frame for audiences the most dramatic, active and/or breathtaking portions in scenes of broad outdoor areas, be they mountains, plains, or deserts. Likewise, in TV coverage of natural disasters like the flood, the camera chooses the most dramatic shots and likely edits these in a fast-paced sequence with other shots in such a way that energy is heightened. Even nature documentaries featuring the smallest of creatures are edited in such a way as to emphasize action and continuous movement. Because of this, electronically created and televised natural landscapes are more immediate and involving than landscapes framed by the naked eye or in print, painting, or photography. Various digital manipulations and sophisticated electronic image devices allow us to edit, slow down, speed up, and even probe the natural world in ways not possible via print media. However, despite differences between print- and electronic-based media, there are some similarities in landscape creation. In painting, in photography, film, videotape and other digitized means, many of the same aesthetic principles apply (Crawford, 1992). These include the choice of natural and man-made objects (Keppler, 1996), creating depth through choices about including foreground and background objects, framing, adhering to the rule of thirds when choosing where to situate the horizon, and manipulating light to create the right color, contrast, or tone.

A glance through *Popular Photography* magazine gives one access to the secrets of famous landscape photographers who offer recipes for creating landscape portraits using all the techniques described earlier, and who quickly remind amateur photographers that not following the principles may result in a landscape that is visually disturbing. Although photographs offer a glimpse of a single moment in nature/place, the illusion of movement of images on film and videotape allows the gaze to move across the landscape, or to travel around and through it. Because of airplanes and helicopters, the camera can travel even farther, offering a wide variety of perspectives. Yet Zettl (1990) advised that, when situating the horizon within a landscape shot, it is important to keep it steady lest you visually disorient or disturb viewers. Because editing techniques allow for manipulation and nonlinear fragmentation of nature and the environment, electronic media in effect re-create them for visual appeal. No matter what technology is used, visual landscapes are cultural and technological creations. As Schama pointed out, a landscape is ordered nature that has been visually contained. Landscapes require an onlooker's gaze, and in the print-dominant age such a gaze offered control. However, although the electronically produced gaze might offer a sense of removal, it does not necessarily offer control.

LANDSCAPES AND NATIONAL IDENTITY

Visual landscapes are an important component of national identity. Particularly in the Western world, landscape is crucial to an articulation of nationhood (Gruffudd, Daniels, & Bishop, 1991; Schama, 1995). In the United States, the wilderness landscape lives on in the created landscapes of the American west, which function to reinforce sacred, regionally distinct yet nationally shared ideals (e.g., individual freedom, manifest destiny, equality, etc.; see Limerick, 1987; Slotkin, 1992). The landscape paintings of Remington and Russell focused on the west, on westward expansion in particular. Such landscapes were popularized for Americans and helped to create a national sense of the past as well as the future (Osborne, 1992). Images of a romanticized, often agrarian past have helped maintain U.S. national identity, but are also used beyond the U.S. In England the work of noted landscape painter John Constable has been used in various ways through time to re-articulate the idyllic rural English countryside, an ordered, peaceful setting (Daniels, 1991). The Anglican church building is an important pictorial icon of English countryside and village landscapes, as noted by geographers Susanne Seymour and Charles Watkins (1995). It is often featured in materials used for purposes of tourism and promotion. Artists have played a powerful role in the process of interpreting nationhood and in creating the national imagination through their landscape creations, argues Brian S. Osborne (1992). For example, painter Jean-Francois Millet's depiction of the noble peasant were important to articulating French national identity, as were Tom Roberts' paintings of the rugged Australian outback and Thoreau McDonald's paintings of bucolic rural Canada. Osborne also discussed the fact that, in Hitler's Third Reich and Stalin's Marxist-Leninist Soviet Union, certain artistic landscape images were promoted to reinforce a sense of unity. These included bucolic farming images and images of a romanticized past. Today, the heritage industry within any nation plays an important role in preserving past landscapes to benefit contemporary national identity (Gruffudd, Daniels, & Bishop, 1991).

Discussions of nation and national identity are deepened by examining the history of the rise of nation and its correspondence to communication technology, as Innis (1951) and McLuhan (1964) have done. Briefly revisiting the argument laid out in chapter 2, the invention of movable type—the printing press—allowed for the expansion of rule from tribe to nation. Control could then be centralized and kingdoms could become large, contained via bureaucracy. McLuhan argued that for 500 years nation has been the standard politically contained geographic entity made possible by print. National identity, a slightly different concept, refers to the outcome of symbolic means and representations thought to accurately encapsulate the unity or meaning of a nation-state. Schlesinger (1991) pointed out that national identity, although an ambiguous concept, has become a hot button issue in the age of electronic media. In electronic-mediated culture, the concept and significance of nation, like nature, is changing. The means to create, reinforce, or maintain national identity is also changing. We witness through satellite TV and the Internet a complete disregard for national borders and a rethinking of previous national laws regarding trade and communication, as Schlesinger pointed out. We are now concerned with international or global commerce. Common today are questions about what will happen to individual national identities in the age of global communication and commerce. No one knows for sure yet, but clearly electronic media are challenging the older, print-based definitions. What is the substance of that challenge? Do we see remnants of the print-dominant era in our electronic media-dominant era? There is a sense that we do and that older conceptions of place coincide, or perhaps collide, with newer conceptions borne of the electronic media age. Ong (1982) argued that entering the age of secondary orality means we bring with us what we learned and experienced in the print-based age. In other words, the emerging acoustic age is not a complete return to the age of orality, but a combination of orality with a reference to literacy. In that sense, nation is the standard we use to define or contemplate the postnation era. The nation, a potent concept as Osborne pointed out, remains with us as do the remnants of national identity as created again and again in landscapes and regional mythologies.

MIDWEST NATURAL LANDSCAPES

A dominant conception of the American midwest heartland landscape is the pastoral ideal most clearly outlined in the previous chapter as the myth of the agrarian midwest. Some of the myth's central visual signifiers or icons are the prairie, croplands, farm structures, gently rolling hills, and waterways (Fry, 1995; Motz, 1981). Two particularly significant midwest icons are the family farm and the Mississippi River. The family farm and its continued resurgence in cultural forms was discussed extensively in chapter 3. Many artists like Grant Wood reinforced the family farm ideal. Wood, who is best known for his American Gothic, created numerous idyllic landscapes of Iowa farmland during the 1930s, when the regionalist style became prevalent largely in response to the heavily industrialized east, urbanization, and the Great Depression (Roberts et al., 1995). Wood clearly set out in his work to celebrate the pastoral as he conceived it. His paintings, revered by some, have by others been called too static or stylized because of their reductionist qualities and romanticized portrayal of the agrarian landscape (Dennis, 1998). A rich icon of the midwest is the major hydraulic artery that runs through the middle of the country. The mighty Mississippi, Old Man River, has long been the subject of story and song (Dorson, 1983). It has been the nation's natural and ideological boundary between the east and west and, for over 100 years, has been a major conduit of commercial shipping. Midwest regionalist painters like contemporary artist John Bloom have devoted their artistic talents to capturing this river of lore, further extending its mythic reach and solidifying its reputation as an important, recognizable midwest landscape. Mark Twain successfully romanticized the Mississippi River in his novels *The Adventures of Huckleberry Finn* and *Tom Sawyer*, but in *Life on the Mississippi* (1917), he recounted his days working on the river and was clear about the realities of the river—its hardships and power. Today the Mississippi River, a major conduit for shipping and tourism, is manipulated by a complex series of locks and dams running from St. Paul, Minnesota, to St. Louis, Missouri, and by over 1,600 miles of main-stem levees as well as a series of cut-offs to shorten its route to the Gulf (Barry, 1997; McPhee, 1989). More and more farms, as noted previously, are now corporate units for international food production. Despite this, in many paintings, works of literature, and other cultural forms, both have been mythologized to the point that utilitarian, economic functions and realities are obscured.

These mythic icons—the farm and The River—are specifically subjects for landscapes constructed in a variety of cultural forms, including journalism. Television journalism in particular relies on the aesthetics and ideological short-hand of mythic landscape—whether of the midwest or other mythic regions or settings—to set the context of particular stories. The author recalled a casual discussion with a young field reporter at the local CBS affiliate in Des Moines, Iowa wherein the reporter relayed the frustration of local stations during the Iowa caucuses held every 4 years prior to the U.S. presidential election. During a recent election, the reporter was asked to supply visiting network correspondents with filler shots for their evening broadcasts from Iowa. She continuously was asked for what she described as *hogs and windmills* shots. Despite voicing her reluctance to help them pictorially reinforce the stereotype, the networks insisted such footage would best signify Iowa.[2] Icons and familiar, stereotyped landscape features are commonly used on TV news. They set a particular context as well as a visual agenda.

TELEVISED DISASTER LANDSCAPES AND THE TRAVELER'S GAZE

During the summer of 1993, the Mississippi River and its many tributaries flooded the banks and levees built to contain them. The flooding was called a *major disaster* and was televised as such. National TV news presented the flood mostly as a conflict between humans and nature. Reporters and anchors made verbal reference to the battle on the Mississippi and the fight between "man (sic) and nature." However, words were only one means to represent the flood. The news cameras were especially adept at framing images of a pastoral midwest landscape turned chaotic. Cameras captured flood footage, while still-store graphic images and computer-generated maps reinforced the sense of mythic place constructed on videotape. This powerful combination of visuals was particularly notable in network TV news.

[2]The discussion took place at KCCI with production assistant Lisa Molina on July 17, 1996.

Because ABC, CBS, and NBC network news headquarters are in New York City, the hovering televisual gaze was decidedly that of the northeast looking to the midwest. Network news teams can be compared with travelers obsessed with looking at and constructing the other in the places to which they travel from home base—New York. In the position of power, travelers observe the people and environments of distant places and create communications about them from travelers' own perspectives, which become, in their communication, the standard or norm. The others that travelers observe—the people and their surroundings—are framed as different, outside that norm. In the act of representing these others in writing, in photos, or on film and videotape, travelers exert a type of voyeuristic control. Geographer Smith (1993) argued that landscapes position viewers as detached voyeurs. In discussing the privileged position of the writers and readers of Gothic romance novels that made extensive use of the traveler format, Saglia (1996) used the term *literary travelers*. He suggested that in these works, "Ultimately, it [the literary landscape] is a site of conflict between the observer's overwhelming desire for control and the subversive chaotic forces of difference" (p. 27). Geographer Tuan (1974) was also concerned with difference, particularly the different visions of tourist and native. He suggested that the voyeuristic gaze of the tourist is one-dimensional, perhaps preconceived. He wrote:

> . . . only the visitor (and particularly the tourist) has a viewpoint; his perception is often a matter of using his eyes to compose pictures. The native, by contrast, has a complex attitude derived from his immersion in the totality of his environment. The visitor's viewpoint, being simple, is easily stated. (p. 63)

John Jakle (1987) argued that landscapes are sign systems. They are images of place meaning, and tourists to a particular area are often in search of the sites for what they deem appropriate landscapes. They search the landscape, he said, for place cues. Where is the right place to take a photograph? What most resembles what I have seen before, elsewhere?

One may ask whether, unlike readers of a novel or tourists who physically travel to a place, TV viewers as tourists are less detached, more immediately involved with the televisual landscape. Viewers must fill in a lot of information that is missing from the screen. They do not get a full, comprehensive view, nor do they get to make visual choices for themselves. Their vision is predetermined and manipulated at the outset by a series of shots that are carefully framed and paced and made to appear spontaneous. Their gaze is completely constructed and technologically enhanced for them while still appearing to some degree natural or at least representative of what they might witness with the naked eye. The real power of the televisually constructed gaze is that it appears natural or representational to the experienced viewer. Zettl (1998) and Meyrowitz (1998), both interested in issues of media literacy, discussed the importance of analyzing not only TV content, but also TV production aesthetics (as Zettl referred to them) or to the grammar of TV (as Meyrowitz referred to it). In other words, both argued that, without a thorough understanding of how sound, camera use, editing, and other technological enhancements are used to create TV, there cannot be a real understanding of the medium as a tool used for good or ill. To be literate in the medium is to understand how TV works on various levels, including the technical level. Here the interest is on the visual production aesthetics coupled with the icons or content of TV flood news, and how together they constructed a mythic place, an epic event, and a way of gazing on it.

Network flood stories all began in New York studios, which is home base from which network correspondents (and vicariously viewers) traveled elsewhere—in this case to the midwest. During flood coverage, the network news cameras captured from a northeast coast perspective the midwestern landscape and the conflict between man and nature. As they constructed that landscape, they also attempted to exert a type of visual control over nature, which had violated the mythic heartland ideal by turning chaotic. This allowed viewers to become travelers to this place, gazing on the midwestern other.[3] Although news cameras created midwest landscapes, they reinforced the need to dominate, yet revere, nature as a separate force. In other words, TV news cameras captured the flood's destruction, but from a safe enough distance—usually from above—to remain out of harm's way, giving the illusion of control. Yet control was not obtained. Television more successfully delivered spectacle. The pictures framed by news cameras and edited for the newscast were aesthetically pleasing, awe-inspiring, yet disturbing landscapes of disaster.

CREATING LANDSCAPES IN TV FLOOD NEWS

The aesthetic conventions of landscape creation were used to portray the flood in various stages of its unfolding. What follows is a description

---

[3]Viewers in the midwest, especially in the most heavily affected areas, received all of the local flood coverage, which was different in many ways from the national coverage. Yet they were still national viewers in that they saw the same network news along with the rest of the country each evening. In that respect, they were given the same network perspective on themselves.

and analysis of network news extreme long shots and graphics used during network flood coverage from early summer 1993 through spring 1994, some local coverage during that period, and postflood documentaries, most of which were produced after the flood. This analysis reveals a set of conventions for creating aesthetic landscapes. It also shows how this coverage created context and how computer-generated graphics aided both video landscape and context in situating the disaster in the heartland, and in forcing network news viewers to adapt to a northeastern national perspective.

The most salient feature of all flood coverage on TV was the extreme long shot (EL shot) taken by cameras in helicopters hovering above flooded rivers, farms, and communities. Normally the range of shot lengths regularly employed in TV news are variations on the close-up, medium close-up, and medium shots. Typically, TV news cameras choose an intimate distance from which to shoot their subjects. A natural disaster such as the flood is a case where the conventions of camera use are stretched to accommodate and create visual spectacle. Extreme long shots were used almost nightly as the flood unfolded. These shots offered framed birds' eye views of water spreading across the flood plains. In both the form and content of these shots—the content and aesthetic cues—one can recognize the rules for creating landscapes as well as the familiar icons of the pastoral midwest. What follows is a description of the TV production techniques of dimensionality, iconography, and dynamism. These techniques are used in all TV production; flood news coverage was no exception. However, highlighting their use in flood coverage is a useful way to emphasize TV's disaster landscape aesthetic.

Dimensionality

During the early stages of flood coverage, from late June through July 1993, the news cameras created landscapes by following the principles of foregrounding and backgrounding subjects to create depth and dimension. Zettl (1990) used the term *Z-axis* to describe where objects are placed within a shot to create depth, or three-dimensional space on the two-dimensional screen. Some of the EL shots also created a sense of heightened energy by tilting the horizon in many shots that panned the earth below. This technique, according to Zettl, creates a disorientation among viewers and a dynamic tension. One especially notable shot appeared on the July 7, 1993, NBC broadcast. NBC frequently used shots like this, with reporter in the helicopter, presented at a slightly tilted angle, and situated frame right, with the water and land below background left. This sort of asymmetrical framing, giving the illusion of depth, is a technique that has been used in landscape painting and pho-

Reporter in helicopter

tography, as discussed earlier, and is used often in TV and other video productions. Because the shot was taken from high above the flood, viewers were offered a sense of visual control, albeit discomforted by the horizontal tilt. The reporter, safe in the helicopter, pointed out the door to the chaos that reigned below. Adding to the energy of the shot and the chaotic atmosphere was the need for the reporter to speak very loudly to be heard above the whirring helicopter blades visible in shadow as they moved across the frame. This additional sound added to the tension. The scene was unsettling, yet knowing the reporter was removed from what was happening provided reassurance that the news teams—and by extension the viewers—were removed from the chaos while still able to experience it in its immediate unfolding. The majority of network TV news stories about the flood included helicopter shots, as did most local coverage. Not all of them included the reporter in the helicopter on camera, but all included the reporter's voice-over, speaking from the position of one looking down on the flood from that height, offering a sense of immediacy and involvement with the spectacle below.

Dynamism

Other means by which the TV camera worked to establish context and create dynamic visuals was through zooms, edits, and height. One technique used frequently was focusing on one object or scene, then slowly zooming out to show the extent of water coverage around it. On July 22,

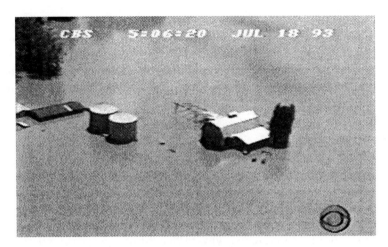

Aerial farm shot

1993, NBC's field report featured a roaming helicopter shot of Illinois' Kaskaskia Island area, which had been completely flooded. One shot began as a close-up of the open, flooded garage of one home, then slowly zoomed out to the entire flooded island in which it was situated. Another dynamic technique used was to start with a wide angle shot from above, then slowly zoom in on one farm, one building, or one stretch of levee. On the July 23 NBC report, the news camera captured in EL shot the flooding water surrounding the small town of Portage des Sioux, Illinois, then zoomed in on the offending broken levee. Later in that same report, the camera zoomed from an EL shot above onto a lone rowboat and oarsman making his way through what were once the streets of Portage des Sioux. In NBC's Kaskaskia Island coverage, cameras panned the area, sometimes covering it at a 360-degree angle. Doing so offered viewers the widest possible perspective on the flood landscape. Zettl (1981) argued that, because of the small size of the TV screen, this deductive approach is not nearly as effective as it is on film. He contended that TV works most effectively if it presents bits of information, in inductive sequence, moving from close-up to close-up. Nevertheless, in the case of the flood, TV news was challenged to portray not only the close-up details, but also the larger landscape. Consequently, a unique dynamic was created. In the panorama mentioned earlier, the water was standing still, not rushing, and no rain was falling. The movement and energy were almost solely creations of the helicopter and camera. To add still more energy, the panorama and long shots, like so many others throughout the tenure of coverage, were nearly always intercut with ground-level footage in fast-paced editing sequences. For example, one sequence of CBS' July 12 Hannibal, Missouri flood coverage featured an aerial shot of the town and surrounding area, followed by a few long shots of the city at ground level, then medium close shots of interview subjects, followed finally by more pans of the area. Edited sequences like these were used all of the time in local and national flood coverage. They functioned to impart an enormous amount of visual information, and also to create a sense of overwhelming urgency.

Iconography

Framed within these panorama and long shots, the subjects of the dynamic tensions on the screen were familiar icons of the midwest: the Mississippi River, farm buildings, crop fields that looked like grids and patches in various stages of growth and flooding, farmers, long stretches of snakelike levee systems, windmills, church steeples, and roads and rural railroad tracks suddenly cut off by flood water. On July 25, 1993, NBC's report from Prairie du Rocher, Illinois, included aerial shots that focused on the broken Sny levee, farm buildings, and the Union Pacific Railroad tracks; ABC's report of July 17, 1993, included a sequence of shots, focusing first on an individual farm windmill, then another farm, then a stretch of rural road connecting Illinois and Missouri across the Mississippi River. The postflood CBS Evening News report of November 7 featured the small town of Hardin, Illinois, and its surrounding farm area. A sequence of shots at the beginning of the newscast featured ruined farmhouses, barns and silos, still-soaked farm fields, and the quiet small town streets of Hardin. Documentary flood coverage was filled with the same familiar imagery. The CBS *I Remember* piece included many, many farm shots, from above and on the ground, lots of churches, and lots of flags. Icons like these dotted the TV news landscape for months during the flood and for a time thereafter. As stable, recurring images, they provided a means by which to measure the relative spread of the water surrounding them, and they also established the context of a pastoral setting now threatened by nature's destructive course.

MAPS AND STILL STORES

Computer-generated graphics inserted into all of the TV news coverage reinforced the disaster landscape aesthetic produced in video footage. Numerous different graphic maps and still store images provided visual variety as well as ideological continuity of the agrarian myth. They also placed the flood in cartographic context. On almost every single newscast, all three networks used box still store or over-the-shoulder graphics

Stillstore image

to visually signal the story. These graphics typically appeared above and to the right of the anchor as he or she announced the evening's midwest flood update prior to the report from the field. Much like product labels, many of the still stores had the character-generated words "Great Midwest Flood" or "Heartland Flood" running across the bottom while the middle and top portions of the graphic frame featured basic heartland iconography. The CBS box still stores featured throughout most of the flood coverage were either a barn with a windmill next to it (as seen, e.g., in the July 18 report) or a stretch of river flowing diagonally next to a prairie or a barn (as seen in the July 20 report). ABC's still stores, such as the one used for the June 30 report, regularly included a white farmhouse or a farm field landscape. NBC also preferred a graphic featuring the white farmhouse and the words, "The Great Flood of '93" in bold letters next to it in many of its still stores, an example of which appeared in NBC's August 7 report. These still store graphics not only reinforced a heartland-gone-wrong concept, but also gave viewers a regional frame of reference. Although the landscapes in the still stores aided viewers to recall the *mythic* where of the disaster, maps used in news stories directed viewers to the *geographic* where.

Landscapes are one form of place representation; maps are another. Maps are place representations with agendas all their own. A map is to place what a clock is to time. It is a measure as well as a visual representation of space from a particular perspective. Maps tell a story all their own. The history of cartography is a fascinating tale of changes in world views and communications media, of conquests, and of the ultimate triumph of scientific positivism and capitalism (Mukerji, 1984). In his detailed history of the development of news cartography, Monmonier (1989) examined how the use of maps in various news media have influenced the development of perceptions of foreign, domestic, and local problems. The news media, he argued, are society's "most significant cartographic gatekeeper and its most influential geographic educator" (p. 19). Grid cartography, a product of print-dominant culture, with its straight clean lines, place names, and visual perspective, denies the histories of national and tribal struggles. These maps visually sanitize. Literary critic Beebee (1995), for example, argued that the continental United States represented on a map as 48 contiguous united states suggests past and present unity while denying the country's real history of struggles and strife. The map, he said, supports a grand ideological narrative of the nation. Maps used in TV news are often fragmented depictions, ahistorical, and presented without a larger context. Typically the only context is that placed around them within the news story.

Local news flood coverage included detailed maps that were of practical use to local viewers. Such maps provided information about closed roads and other areas closed off to residents, commuters, and travelers. Local viewers could rely on these to help them plan daily activities. Yet in network flood coverage, maps were used in most stories to highlight areas that were the focus of the day's flood news, but more broadly to reinforce a particular network/viewer gaze. Close analysis of network news stories indicates that the gaze constructed through the aid of news maps originated in the U.S. northeast. As illustrated in the following examples, what was included in the maps and how they moved on the screen reinforced a northeastern perspective moving to the midwest.

Most flood reports from the field began with a computer-generated map that situated the geographic origin of the story. Although by mid- to late-summer, regular viewers were clear about where in the United States the flood was taking place, maps were featured at the beginning in most broadcasts and throughout individual news reports.[4] The introductory maps used on all three networks constructed a preferred gaze on the midwest. NBC began many of its flood stories with two maps on the screen, one across the bottom left, the other, larger map situated above in the middle of the screen. For example, on August 9, the lower map was of the contiguous United States, the larger map (an

---

[4]Introductory maps were often used as the anchor introduced the story; then when the story moved to location, field reports also included slightly more detailed maps of the area or areas covered within the story.

enlarged inset of the map below it) included only the midwestern states along the Mississippi River. The context—the entire United States in the smaller map—situated the viewer's gaze away from the coasts and toward the heartland territory of the country. A more blatantly eastern gaze was constructed in the maps used frequently on CBS and ABC. In the June 28 reports on both of these networks, the opening map was of one half of the continental United

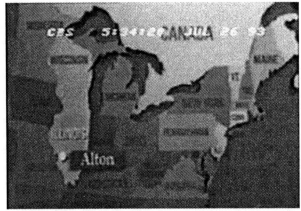

Map 1

States. The Mississippi River states appeared screen left, the Mid-Atlantic coastal states screen right. Highlighted on the right was New York City and on the left the particular area along the Mississippi River or other river site that was the focus of that evening's disaster report. One implication of this, again, was that the midwest needed to be placed within a larger context for the viewer to understand where the disaster was taking place. The maps guided the viewer (as did the network newscasters) on a journey from New York City, the CBS news headquarters, to the nation's heartland. The way in which the map sometimes appeared on screen was most interesting. The eastern section of the United States appeared first, then a visual sweep to the left revealed the rest of the map that stopped at the Mississippi River states. It would be hard to imagine a more clearly constructed eastern gaze than this. These news maps were setting a visual travel agenda for

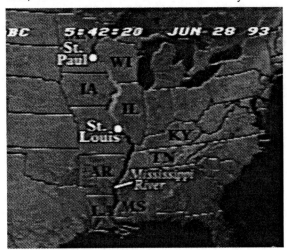

Map 2

viewers, readying their eyes for the onscreen corruption of nature that awaited once they arrived. Interviews with David Abbate, the art director in the graphics department at CBS, and with NBC graphics producer Paul Hammons, reveal that neither had really thought about why the partial map was used and why the East Coast was included as it was in maps of the midwest (personal communication, July 28, 1997). Abbate said he assumed that people were just used to seeing the East Coast, which reinforces the idea that the East Coast, and especially New York City, is the implied center of news reality partly because of the network news headquarters there.

Interviews with these network graphics personnel in New York—where all the still store images and maps are generated for the network newscasts—also reveal that less time is spent fussing over the content of these graphics and much more on meeting tight deadlines and achieving the appropriate overall graphic look that must be uniform throughout the newscast. Both graphics personnel spent quite a bit of time discussing the importance of what all the graphics look like and how that look changes occasionally to keep viewers visually interested in the news, and to keep up with changes in graphic software available to create special effects. With regard to network flood coverage, one might attribute the narrow range of icons chosen for still stores, and the way maps contextualized the midwest, to the routines of TV journalism, the deadlines of TV in general, and to the fact the New York is the center of broadcast network news production. New York is the place from which senior and executive producers dictate visuals, and graphics departments carry out their wishes. Although producing and distributing news from the center to the periphery in this way is efficient, closer analysis of these visuals raises questions about the subtle powers of the northeastern perspective (as center) and the concomitant reinforcement of place meanings. Hay (1993) argued that TV networks create their own geographies and their own sense of space. Certainly in this instance a spatial hierarchy is made clear in the way maps and other graphics were used with video footage.

THE QUINTESSENTIAL DISASTER LANDSCAPE

The much-referenced footage of the August 1 farmhouse dismantling, as detailed at the beginning of the chapter, can now be placed in the larger context of TV flood news aesthetics. The August 1 shot included the most prevalent of midwest icons, the farmhouse. The power of the water rushing through the broken levee literally crushed the house and surrounding structures. What made this shot unique in terms of TV news aesthetics was that so much energy was in the subject and did not need to be added by camera zooms, edits, or tilts of the horizon. Yet these were used, albeit more subtly than in other footage. News personnel had a choice about how to capture the event and how the audience should gaze on this spectacle. The shot opened the flood news segment on ABC and NBC and was the second item on CBS. All three networks included a map at the beginning of coverage; on all three, the map consisted of only the midwest states on the screen with either the states of Missouri and Illinois highlighted, or only Missouri. The Mississippi and Missouri Rivers were prominent on all of the maps. These maps signaled the geographical setting of the day's flood news. Then all dissolved into video footage. The farm dismantling image was necessarily shot from above. Because of helicopters, the camera could hover above the farmhouse and move with the river. The camera lens could zoom in or out on the farmhouse, could frame it tightly in the shot, or could add another building or stretch of the swiftly flowing water. Different stations made different technical choices, but the effect was similar: constant movement, continuous tension and continuous emphasis on that farmhouse.

   After its initial broadcast, inclusion of the crumbling farmhouse in subsequent news stories and flood documentaries was a testament to the significance of the event and the influence of editing. It had enormous aesthetic appeal as a beautiful and dramatic piece of footage. It also had tremendous ideological appeal—the horror of heartland destruction by a previously passive natural force. The beautiful and the horrid, captured in such concentrated form, was offered to viewers as a scene from a much larger flooding landscape. In fact, at the time, many other farms close by were also destroyed immediately after, but none with the same dramatic effect. This small piece of the larger disaster landscape was offered over and over again, edited in with other footage, confusing linear time sequence, creating its own time. The visual impact of this landscape was immediate, dramatic, and absorbing. These few moments both chronicled and created the height of chaos wrought by nature's destruction on the heartland. Daily coverage thereafter focused visually on repairing this landscape.

ROMANTICIZING THE LANDSCAPE

Specific uses of light, framing, and focus were particularly noticeable strategies used in visual coverage of the flood to recover or reassert the heartland myth. Many shots, especially those that opened and closed follow-up reports from flood-torn areas of the midwest, featured the still river or desolate farmland lit by the sun low in the sky at dusk or visible on the upper screen and reflected beautifully in the river. On March 18, 1994, on CBS' *Eye on America* report, this took the form of a full sunset shot, with the orange and pink hues of light splashing across the water. Part of the farm—the barn and windmill—were situated frame left. Connotatively, this landscape suggested the bucolic heartland had renewed, although slightly worse for wear. A return to the pastoral myth was also constructed through the use of soft focus. The framing of the slow renewal of desolate farm lands, the destroyed barns, and the deserted streets of some small towns—church steeples and all—was enabled partly through their visual treatment as fuzzy edged land-scapes. On the October 14th ABC *American Agenda* report, these icons were asymmetrically framed in aesthetically pleasing fashion; from an overhead shot of a steady horizon, the soft focus landscape nostalgically evoked the enduring heartland myth. The end of the *Nova* flood docu-mentary included numerous shots of sunlit prairies, farmlands, and rivers. The purpose of the final images was to show where the land was after the flood. In some shots, the land was beautifully green; in others, the farm fields especially, the land looked devastated. Trees without leaves stood out alone in sandy fields. Although there were obvious negative changes, the images were beautifully lit and beautifully com-posed. They appeared at rest, peaceful. In all of these postflood images the camera work reinforced the heartland as a bucolic landscape reassur-ing viewers that nature had settled down and all was returning to nor-mal. Land and waterways would reemerge as productive minions of

Destroyed farm 1

Destroyed farm 2

human will, and the heartland myth could endure, albeit altered by the logic of TV.

Analyzing TV news visuals in isolation is a first step in understanding how the camera and other graphic elements work not merely to reinforce shared meanings of places and events, but in fact to create them. Television news created a flood event that unfolded in a mythic place and time. Each type of TV news visual employed in flood coverage—videotape footage, still store images, and maps—were fragmented, presented out of context, and aesthetically enhanced to conform to the dictates of drama and tension on the small screen. Editing techniques allowed for the flood to unfold in fragmented sequence, especially in late-stage flood reporting and flood documentaries. The flood was an epic that unfolded in what Newcomb (1982) called mythic, sacred time. Newcomb argued that part of the aesthetic of TV is its unique sense of history. Television news appointed a beginning and end to the flood, and the editing of flood footage meant that, visually, the flood did not unfold in linear fashion, but moved back and forth from stage to stage and site to site. On the one hand, this raises serious questions about journalism and objectivity. On the other hand, it is an example of TV living up to its aesthetic potential. Zettl (1980) specifically discussed the peculiar temporal aspects of TV. He argued that we must "place the medium in the context of some of the prevailing experiential phenomena of our time: the instantaneousness of the moment, the complexity of experience, and the multiplicity of viewpoint" (p. 127). Zettl clearly focused on what TV can do best.

In a larger view, one may ask, is TV, doing what it does best, the major *reason* for these prevailing experiential phenomena? Do we prefer the dramatic landscapes offered on TV because they are compressed, fragmented, and filled with tension? Do such visual landscapes inform our visual experiences away from the screen? Is TV time—multidimensional, nonlinear, focused on the here and now—a preferred way to experience time in general? Certainly these questions go beyond the flood, and the answers may vary from place to place (and perhaps culture to culture). Yet there are specific implications for televised flood coverage and for TV natural disaster news in general. It seems that a focus on TV visuals, the content as well as the aesthetics, forces one to recognize how nature and place are transformed on and for the small screen. The manipulations of the camera, the use of computer-generated maps and graphics, and the infrastructure of network TV are elements of change. However, the chosen iconography and theme of restoring the nation's bucolic heartland are elements of continuity. In TV news, change and continuity collide. The heartland, a mythic place, is made fluid, malleable to cultural practice and especially to communication technology. Here TV created a unique sense of geography and history, as TV does in all natural disaster coverage. That generally we accept TV's portrayals of nature and place, and the gaze constructed for us, indicates that the medium has indeed altered our perspective.

4

Local Versus National Flood News

Television potentially performs a number of services during natural disaster. It can predict oncoming natural forces, describe damages, and even act as a community bulletin board—informing those in the immediate area and beyond how to get relief, how to assist in the relief effort, and whether friends and family are safe. Yet many of these services are performed by local news organizations, not the networks. This chapter looks at how TV news organizations, and specifically news staff—primarily reporters—carry out their journalistic duty during natural disaster situations. The chapter also questions the concept of journalistic duty within the context of the medium of TV. Although government agencies, communication scholars, and other social scientists have carried out research on how the media perform or should perform during a natural disaster, only some of the research discusses specifically TV news, and much of it only partially includes a number of important aspects of disaster coverage, such as how reporters are challenged during disaster coverage and the geographic significance of the news itself (Garner, 1992; see also Carter, 1980; Christensen & Ruch, 1978; Kreps, 1980; Medsger, 1989; Quarantelli, 1989; Raphael, 1986; Rogers & Sood, 1980).

First, it is important to look at how journalists actually approach and react to reporting a major natural disaster. Second, it is important to differentiate between network and local reporters and news organizations when discussing how TV news performs during natural disasters. The two groups have separate obligations, separate audiences, and they take different types of risks. All of them face occupational threats, but local news staff bear an added threat to family, friends, and personal property, not to mention the communities to which they belong. News staff on the scene at the flood had a job to do. That job was to cover it as a major news event. Yet the flood was not a typical news event. It was a situation that personally and professionally affected how reporters and other news personnel did their jobs. In some ways, covering the flood of 1993 was like covering a war. Because it was so long in unfolding, and because it caused so much turmoil over such a large geographic area, it was a burdensome and sometimes unsafe and unhealthy undertaking.

Another flood in the midwest, the severe spring flooding in the Red River Valley in northern Minnesota and North Dakota in 1997, did not last quite as long, nor did it cover as much territory as did the 1993 flood. However, it had a similar impact and received significant local and national news coverage. Hardest hit in that flood were Grand Forks, North Dakota, and East Grand Forks, Minnesota. The three networks came to cover that flood during one especially crucial weekend, April 18 to 20, when blizzard conditions, flooding, and a major fire converged on the dual cities.

Although both disasters were widely covered on TV, the network coverage differed from the local coverage. The difference had to do not only with the type of information broadcast—the content—but also with the overall function of local news versus network news. The focal question explored in this chapter is: what is the geographic significance of televised natural disaster news? More specifically, What should be the role of the local news broadcast in instances of natural disaster? What should be the role of the national network broadcast? What roles did local and national news play during the midwest floods of 1993 and 1997? What impact did local and national flood broadcasts have on the region and nation? What was the impact on reporters and other news personnel? What are the prescribed duties of journalists during a natural disaster? What duties did local and network journalists perform? What ethical considerations arise when covering a natural disaster? Finally, how does the medium of TV figure into a discussion of ethics, obligations, and actual practice of news organizations during natural disaster?

To answer these questions, this chapter discusses a number of areas: how TV reporters and news stations were affected during the 1993 and 1997 floods; the extent to which each could and did rely on established formulas or conventions for newsgathering and reporting; the prevalence of established news frames; recommendations made about how news should handle instances of disaster; and, finally, whether such recommendations do, or can possibly apply, to TV news.

IMPACT OF FLOOD ON LOCAL AND NATIONAL NEWS PERSONNEL

How did local and on-the-scene network reporters cope with these floods in their professional capacities as newsgatherers? How were they personally affected? When asked to recall their experiences covering the floods, local and network reporters and other news personnel had vivid memories. It seems that during these two floods, at stake for them, in varying degrees, were: threatened and actual loss of facilities for news-gathering and broadcasting; disruption of their personal routines; their health, the health and safety of loved ones; and damage to personal property.

ABC network correspondent Erin Hayes recounted her problems in Grand Forks, North Dakota, in 1997 (personal communication, July 24, 1997). WDAZ, the ABC affiliate there, had given the network crew a room in which to set up their equipment and work. Hayes talked about how spooky it was to drive into Grand Forks as everyone else was evacuating, and how fast the water was rising and spilling into city streets. After they were set up at WDAZ a while, flood waters threatened the station, and eventually the network had to pick up and leave to broadcast from someplace else.

CBS correspondent Vickie Mabrey described what she called the CBS *worldwide flood headquarters* set up in the Holiday Inn in Alton, Illinois—just outside St. Louis—during the 1993 flood (personal communication, July 9, 1997). The water treatment plant in Alton had flooded, so no one had water for anything. There were no showers, no laundry, no toilets, and there was no drinking water, she said. Everyone in the crew had to drink the bottled water CBS flew in especially for their crews.

Another CBS correspondent, Scott Pelle, spent a good deal of time covering the 1993 flood in the Des Moines, Iowa area. He, too, talked about how CBS brought in water for crews when the Des Moines water treatment plant flooded and all of the stores were sold out of bottled water (personal communication, July 7, 1997). He added that remote crews and correspondents are used to having supplies, including food, electricity, and other kinds of equipment essential to newsgathering, shipped in when there are problems with the local infrastructure.

WDAZ, in Grand Forks, almost shut down in 1997, but workers were able to sandbag enough on one side of the station's building that they could remain operating there—under Army National Guard surveillance. Just in case they would be completely flooded out, the station set up a news operating base in nearby Honeyford, North Dakota, a town that local reporter Terry Dullum described as a few houses and a grain elevator (personal communication, July 8, 1998). The backup location never had to be used for full-station operations, he said, but he did some live remotes from the fully operating grain elevator. Since citizens of Grand Forks knew that the WDAZ news crew was not able to leave the station, they brought hot dishes to keep the news team going.

At KCCI in Des Moines, flooding at the station in 1993 caused not only the loss of water, but also a complete power shutdown. The station was able to transmit news by using emergency generators and broadcast equipment flown in from Minneapolis, Minnesota. Staff interviewed at the station said they were operating under very dim lights for a number of days (Staff interviews at KCCI took place on July 17, 1996). And because many staff members couldn't leave the station, people living in the area who were able to get to the station brought food and water to nourish the news crew.

New Director Mike Brue, at WDAZ, said that on a number of occasions during the 1997 flood he had to plead with Army National Guardsman to let him cross the bridge over the Red River with videotapes of flood damages in Minnesota for broadcast (personal communication, July 6, 1998). Guardsman were worried, he said, about the safety of the bridge under threatening flood conditions.

Although all reporters were faced with having to cope with the problem of the inability to operate at full capacity at the local stations and in the local setup headquarters, a number also faced threats to health and safety and were inconvenienced in their personal lives. Some reporters had an easier time coping with the inconvenience than did others. Some did not have to do so.

Both Erin Hayes and Vickie Mabrey said they became ill from toxic flood water during the 1993 flood—something suffered by many people living in the flooded areas. After reporting a few weeks on the 1997 flood, Hayes also said she became so physically exhausted that she finally had to pack up and leave. When asked how she made the decision to finally go, she answered, "You know when you're groggy and you're forgetting things and you forget where you are when you wake up . . . if it takes you ten minutes after you wake up to remember where you are . . . you know you've gone too long."

Kenley Jones, a veteran correspondent with NBC, said he made the decision to stop reporting the 1993 flood from where he was based near St. Louis when his vacation time came (personal communication, July 11, 1997). There was no conflict for him—he just left.

When the CBS crew in Alton, Illinois, ran out of water, most of them just suffered through without showers. Yet Vickie Mabrey confessed that her parents live in nearby St. Louis, Missouri, and when she had a day off she would go there and shower and do her laundry.

Local reporters and news crews didn't have many options—certainly not attractive ones--regarding how long they got to cover the floods and under what conditions. They could not take breaks to suit their personal schedules or needs. Much more than the network reporters, local reporters' personal lives were affected.

At KCCI in Des Moines, a number of reporters told stories about how they were going about their private lives when they were suddenly called to work during another unexpected flash flooding. Anchor and reporter Kevin Cooney left his home on a Saturday morning to get doughnuts for his family. It was taking a while for him to return, and his wife, anxiously waiting for him, was watching KCCI news on TV. Suddenly, there on the screen, was Cooney doing a live report from one of the areas hit hardest. The station called his car phone and he did not have time to contact his family. Similarly, KCCI reporter Sarah Jarvis had a weekend off after a long stretch of nonstop coverage. Water was still unavailable in Des Moines, so Jarvis was driving to her parents' home in Minneapolis to do laundry and rest. She barely got out of Des Moines when she, too, was called to do an emergency live remote in the pouring rain wearing little clothing.

Mike Brue, news director at WDAZ in Grand Forks, said he had to sleep at the station for almost a week during the worst part of the 1997 flooding. The reason was not only the round-the-clock coverage, but also because his home in Alvaredo, Minnesota could only be reached via major detours. Normally only a few minutes from Grand Forks over the Red River, his home by detour was about 290 miles away.

Besides major inconveniences to their persons, local reporters also had at stake the safety of family, friends, and property. WDAZ reporter Terry Dullum said his condo had to be sandbagged. One night he, his wife, and fellow condo owners sandbagged until three in the morning, then immediately afterward Dullum was off to the station to appear on the air again. Eventually they were evacuated from their home. He said he slept at the station a few nights at that time while his wife stayed with parents. Dullum also reported that the station anchor lost his home completely during the 1997 flood and waited 1 year for federal money to find a new one.

Considering how the floods affected news personnel, both personally and professionally, one must consider the impact that had on the flood news. What became of news routines at this time? Were they altered? To what extent?

Mike Brue described at length how all station employees eventually had to make a decision between staying and working and leaving to assist loved ones or evacuate their own homes. He said it was incredibly stressful, and emotions ran high at the station as employees tearfully made their decision to go. "People are still dealing with the emotional toll," he said as he described the impact of the flood on the entire news crew at the station. Brue explained that the biggest emotional impact on the WDAZ staff came not from personal loss, but from the reaction by residents of nearby communities and states, and even Canada. People were willing to help and called the station continuously to offer such help. Clearly this was an extraordinary experience.

Generally speaking, in many ways, natural disaster news differs from other news only in specific content. Many of the same formulas or conventions for newsgathering and news presentation are present in most TV news stories. Sociologists Tuchman (1978) and Gans (1979) established precedent with their studies on how the press routinely cover events. They argued that, by using similar and consistent frames of understanding to interpret and report on what they consider newsworthy events, news organizations actually create versions of reality. These versions become familiar. Similarly, Nimmo and Combs (1985) argued that, over time, news workers develop standardized ways of gathering and reporting news. Interested specifically in TV news, Nimmo and Combs showed that most TV news organizations share the following: definitions of what is newsworthy, conventions of aesthetic and visual presentation, and similar overall news logic, including order of presentation, visuals, and words. The reasons for standardizing news are clear from an economic standpoint. Standardization saves TV networks and local stations money because it saves time. Audiences have become familiar with predictable reporting formats and find them comfortable, understandable, and thus habit forming to watch. So stations make money via higher ratings. Also commenting on TV news predictability, Griffin (1992) pointed out that TV news tends toward format redundancy in terms of visual choices and overall presentation no matter the news topic. Another predictable element of TV news is its tendency to entertain the audience. Postman and Powers (1992) discussed at length the entertainment functions of TV news and its corresponding economic viability. As early as 1958, Edward R. Murrow chastised TV news for that tendency in an address to the Radio Television News Directors Association (RTNDA), saying that broadcast TV news is basically an incompatible combination of show business, advertising, and news (Goedkoop, 1988). Critic Ron Powers (1980), in his book *The Newscasters*, pointed the finger at local TV news in particular, saying it answers less to the descriptions of journalism and more to that of show business. More recently, PBS examined how nightly news in general has changed, placing much more emphasis on entertainment and less on information in the age of increasing media consolidation (see Storm, 2001).

NEWS FRAMES

News organizations, both print and electronic, routinely frame events in ways that help explain what they are about. According to Gamson (1988), news frames can be thought of as underlying themes that offer a way to interpret or understand a reported event. Most people experienced the midwest floods of 1993 and 1997 only through the news. As a result, news organizations played a powerful role in shaping what and how people understood them. The floods were framed in ways not unlike many disaster stories. Media scholar Garner (1994) examined the news frames used by local and national print news organizations when covering the 1993 flood. The central organizing frame, she found, was the fight with Mother Nature. National print discourse, she argued, focused on what the flood cost the nation. Local print discourse, however, focused on personal loss. Despite their differences, both national and local print organizations framed the flood as a fight with nature. Garner illustrated that theme by citing numerous examples of how battle metaphors were used consistently throughout coverage. Scholars Meeds and Thorson (1994) also examined news frames used in coverage of the 1993 flood, but they examined specifically TV news. Their analysis was limited to 4 weeks of ABC network coverage. Meeds and Thorson found that the most common frames ABC used were: economics, prediction, solidarity and fighting back, devastation, blame and conflict, and helplessness. They briefly discussed the types of images presented on ABC when certain news frames were used. For example, helicopter shots of flooded towns corresponded with the helplessness frame, whereas shots of sandbaggers corresponded with the solidarity and fighting back frame. Meeds and Thorson found that the 1993 flood was framed as a drama, as are most disasters on TV, and that this typical way of framing the flood disaster did not allow for an understanding of the event that would in any way help people who might face such a disaster in the future.

Clearly during both the 1993 and 1997 floods, local and network TV news attempted to make sense of the continuous flooding by employing legitimating frames of reference through which to understand them, and also to restore the idyllic heartland myth. The dominant news frames employed in local and national TV news of these floods

Sandbagging 1

were not unlike those found by Garner and by Meeds and Thorson. The major underlying theme was the fight with Mother Nature. A prevailing war metaphor was employed throughout flood coverage. In fact, it was used to describe the disaster 32 times out of 115 network news stories. According to the news, both network and local, the battles on the Mississippi River were waged between farmers and townsfolk who had worked hard to build successful farms and family businesses only to see nature willfully work to destroy all they had achieved. In the struggle for economic and human survival, midwesterners pulled together, fighting the river with sandbags and through other means, sometimes to no avail.

Although war was a continuous theme throughout, a number of distinct news frames that were frequently employed focused on different aspects of flood experience and control. The subthemes or frames operating under the rubric of the fight with Mother Nature were political-economic controls and correctives, scientific control and explanation, and, finally, aesthetic control. These were not mutually exclusive during flood reports. In fact, the aesthetic dominated most news reports, particularly near the end of network TV news coverage of the 1993 flood. To make sense of the continuous devastation, and to keep stories fresh during this slowly developing natural disaster, TV news often chose to report from the political-economic front. These stories focused on the local and national economic damages, and also described the continual pleas made to local and federal government officials and agencies for monetary aid, official visits, and other help in controlling the waters and evacuating residents, including bringing in Army Reserve troops, further reinforcing a war scenario. Another common frame, the scientific, was evident in those stories which focused on the Army Corps of Engineers and their work on the levees and the elaborate lock and dam system that runs along the Mississippi River. These stories were peppered heavily with shots of computers, maps, and graphs indicating the science or technology involved in river control. Finally, and perhaps most prominent of the three, is the aesthetic frame, which can be described as the way in which broadcast news used visuals and verbal descriptions of the flooding and its consequences in a way that appealed to viewers' sense of the awesome, the beautiful, and the horrid. Camera use, graphics, editing techniques, and other special effects together offered viewers an incredible sensual and dramatic experience of the flood. Because TV is visual above all, the aesthetic frame dominated the form of the news.

It would be difficult, in light of the preceding discussion of TV news and its penchant for entertainment, formulaic reporting, and redundant framing, to envision natural disasters as instances commanding a special or out of the ordinary public service obligation. But are they? What sort of public service should TV news perform during natural disaster? What are the duties of journalists during such times? Are there different obligations among local journalists and news organizations, and network journalists and organizations? Are routines of newsgathering and presentation, and established frames for understanding news, anathema to public service?

NETWORK CORRESPONDENT INTERVIEWS

When asked about the routines of covering the floods, network correspondents indicated that certainly the news routine was unique during the period of flood coverage—to the degree that each disaster poses its own unique challenges—but a certain kind of routine could be established. In the case of the 1993 flood, this was partly due to the sheer length of the disaster. However, based on their own accounts, network news crews did not break in any significant way from established routines for newsgathering and reporting when covering both floods. They stayed within the confines of previously established—although often implicit—guidelines regarding who they relied on for information, how they went about choosing visuals and other elements, how they chose interview subjects, how they framed their stories, and the extent to which they relied on network news executive producers and other news personnel in New York.

The daily routine of the six correspondents interviewed was similar. All of them would begin each day very early. Typically they would contact the local Federal Emergency Management Authority (FEMA) and/or the Army Corps of Engineers or other authorities involved in controlling or reacting to the flood to find out where the action was that day. These official sources were instrumental in directing national news to certain areas or aspects of the flood. Kenley Jones of CBS explained: ". . . yes, we did have contact with the Corps, and they had offices and they had people who were watching it and we would talk to them. We relied on them for a great deal of information, but also local authorities. . . ." Similarly, according to Vickie Mabrey: "We checked with the Army Corps of Engineers. Everyday we talked to them several times and found out who was sandbagging where, who had some local FEMA officials coming in to take a look around, and we would plan, maybe we'll go there. . . "

The daily news routine also included an early ride in the helicopter looking for good visuals and other interesting elements. The helicopter proved an invaluable tool for all of the network news crews covering the flood—not only because with it they could cover a large area in a short time, but also because helicopters offered a visual perspective on the flood that proved particularly enticing to newsgatherers. It seems all of the reporters were interested in capturing the most original and dramatic visual. Vickie Mabrey, John Gibson, Kenley Jones and Scott Pelle all said that part of the routine each day was to get up in the helicopter and start looking around. According to Pelle: "I would go out in the helicopter and look for the key elements, the pivotal interview or scene or something that we could make our own."

Tom Foreman, who covered the flood for the NBC *Today Show*, talked about how they relied on the helicopter. "It was primarily Kenley since he was working for nightly news, and I was doing the *Today Show*. So Kenley and his crew would get up and go. And they'd be gone most of the day. And then . . . they'd go to wherever the hot spot was, which they learned by radio and by cell phone and by looking. And so they'd fly all day. And then most days I would work with their tape but some days I would go when they were back . . . I did weekends where I did the flying around all day."

Mabrey explained that, "Well, we go . . . the helicopter lands in the morning at about eight, we get in the helicopter, we're flying along . . . we're looking for Prairie du Rocher or Ste. Genevieve. We land where we see people sandbagging. We get out, we shoot people sandbagging, talk to them about their stories. . . ."

In describing the value of a dramatic helicopter shot, CBS reporter Scott Pelle recounted,

> Mark [field producer] and I were up in Fargo and the first thing we did, we'd roll out of bed first thing in the morning and go ahead and shoot everything we can shoot. . . . Now I want an element that I can call my own, that will be a sort of fulcrum on which the piece will turn. So I get a helicopter and I go out on a particular day and I'm just looking for targets of opportunity. I don't have any particular idea about where I'm going or what I'm gonna find. But in a disaster situation you're generally going to find something, especially if you're riding around in a helicopter.

Later in the interview, Pelle came back to the importance of the helicopter in his quest for dramatic visuals:

> My mandate from the Evening News that night, this was early in the flood, my mandate that night was, "show me the big picture. Don't show me a neighborhood in West Alton. Give me a couple of hundred miles worth." . . . They wanted a big, sweeping, here we have a historic flood and here's why its historic. They wanted a scope piece that day.

The *they* Pelle was talking about were CBS news executives in New York. Reporters did not make solo decisions about any of the stories they worked on for the networks. When asked about the extent of routine collaboration on each piece, all of the reporters described the number of other news personnel involved in pulling together any one piece on any one day. Reporters worked with at least one and sometimes two or more field producers and editors who made decisions with them about appropriate story ideas, visual choices, and story structure. Each step in the process of putting together a package for the day or evening newscast was a collaborative effort. Reporters' descriptions of the collaborative process suggest that much of what they understood about appropriate choices was implicit, part of what became second nature to them on the job. All of them indicated an understanding that no piece was strictly their own, and that it was important to always be aware of what the networks were looking for.

As Erin Hayes explained,

> Well, I wrote to very specific visuals, and wrote a standup that kind of illustrated it. So, to that degree I blocked out what the primary visual elements would be. And then the producer sat with the editor and made the final decisions. But we both have, its a collaborative

effort. I would never say to the producer, you can't do this and he wouldn't say to me, you can't do this. . . . They [the producer and editor] generally do the final cut.

Regarding input from New York,

There were times when they were aware of things that we might not be aware of—reaction in Washington, or bits of the story that we might not be focused on because we were focused very locally, so, yeah, it's just, it's a collaborative thing. . . . And senior producers that were in New York would ask questions that the average viewer would ask, or would have insight that we hadn't thought of because we were focused very specifically on one thing.

NBC's John Gibson indicated that the network news producers in New York were quite concerned about the text of the story. He explained, "In terms of, was New York making the final decision on pictures, probably not . . . they tend to worry more about the words. They'll go over the script and say, well, what do you mean by this? What do you mean by that?"

Reporters Kenley Jones of NBC and Tom Foreman of ABC also indicated a significant amount of input from the New York news producers. Jones said "Well, that [the decision about the lead story] was determined from the producers in New York . . . the *Nightly News* producers would decide which area they wanted to have the news of the day story."

Foreman described the process this way:

At the network, there tends to be more input from a lot of people. In part because you're trying to do more of a team approach. . . . And ultimately the way the story goes on the air is something . . . we have a great deal of say in crafting what we want to say and how we want to present it. But then, of course, it goes through a group of editors who will then put their own stamp on it. Well, don't do this, or do this and include this. . . . Its mainly, mainly New York, but its a lot of give and take.

All of the reporters discussed the fact that maps and other graphics inserted in their stories were a surprise each day or evening. These were generated in New York and inserted where senior producers thought best to put them.

When asked what they were looking for in story elements, most reporters were clear about what was expected of them. What was expected was something dramatic and spectacular, or at least original.

Erin Hayes, when asked about the extent to which they swapped footage with local stations, indicated that ultimately they [the news crew] were looking for something dramatic, so if the local station had something better than they did, they would go with that.

CBS' Vickie Mabrey explained that they were always looking for character-driven stories. She described one such character.

> Well, I found this guy. . . . Just happened upon him. We did a live shot one morning and he came rowing up in his boat, right after we finished I started talking to him. He seemed like a real outdoorsman, and just kind of a wacky guy, and I said hey, why don't you take us out in your boat? He was absolutely fascinating. He was kind of a little river rat guy . . . and that's what we try to do, is find people who had an interesting story to tell about life along the river. So everyday you try to find a character.

NBC's John Gibson was clear about the network's desire for good pictures. When asked to explain what that was, he answered,

> Something that encapsulates the day. I mean, if it was a day of levee breaks, you'd want to open with levee beaks. If it was a day of sand-bagging and trying to save some place, it would be something like that . . . sometimes you had to make a tough decision about which was the grabbiest picture. If it was a helicopter rescue of somebody off a roof, or a levee actually breaking and blowing up a house.

Sandbagging 2

When asked to explain how they made decisions about what would lead on a day when things seemed to be slow, he explained that,

> . . . on the days when that [the water level] was changing, either dramatically up or dramatically down, I would say that information tended to lead. But there would be other times when it was just high . . . running high and not changing a whole lot. And then it tended to be focused more on some place or person where they had, they were either fighting and they had won, or they were fighting and had lost.

All reporters emphasized, to one degree or another, finding and highlighting the drama no matter what form it happened to take. A focus on drama was also evident in reporters' comments describing how they wrote and structured their scripts, which raised again the issue of choosing visuals, but included how interview subjects were chosen for story inclusion.

All six correspondents said they wrote their scripts to fit the visuals and other elements gathered by their own crews and supplemental crews out on the same news day. Vickie Mabrey said specifically she wrote to the best pictures and sound bites. John Gibson said he was always looking for the strongest picture on which to base his script. When asked specifically about how interview subjects were chosen, Gibson replied that, "When choosing people to interview either to personalize the story or to comment on something that was happening, and they weren't an official, you were always looking for somebody who could encapsulate in the shortest possible bite whatever the situation was."

Many of the reporters interspersed their comments about routine flood reporting with comments about the importance of their reports and the power of TV in a social and political sense, particularly in this instance. As Scott Pelle explained,

> People who think these things through realize there's a tremendous benefit to television news covering natural disasters. The benefit is that the rest of the nation sees how bad it is. That drives appropriations in Congress, it drives the Red Cross, it drives people in Sacramento to send a 10 dollar check to the Red Cross for the people in Des Moines. So there's a tremendous leverage created by the presence of television news, unlike radio, that tells the rest of the country that it's just not another flood, it's not just another blizzard. And people in this country tend to pour their hearts out and their cash. . . . Its [TV disaster coverage] a political imperative. In terms of not just showing Congressman and Senators how bad it is, but it becomes a political imperative because when you put it on the evening news every night, there's a sense in Congress of, ooh, we'd better get on this. We can't ignore this.

With similar zeal, when asked whether she thought network flood stories had a political impact, Vickie Mabrey replied,

> Oh, absolutely. He [President Clinton] can fly over and take a look, but how often is he going to actually come there, fly over and look? Not very often. So he relies on television, on his advisors. But mostly it's seeing the picture and hearing the stories, I think, that makes the difference in how much money people receive. . . . He [Clinton] did come, I guess, twice. And Al Gore came, and Ross Perot even came. But they're not gonna be there everyday. They're not gonna see the magnitude of it for themselves. They really rely on television.

Talking with network correspondents about the logistics and routines of covering the floods, and about how they perceived the importance of their jobs in a larger political and social sense, one realizes that they perceive the routines of newsgathering and reporting—trying to get a dramatic picture and succinct sound bites—as vital. Their job, as they see it, is to continually look for these and to pull the best televisual elements together in collaboration with others—in the field and in New York—so the story will reach its audience and appropriate understanding and help will result. In a sense, there seemed to be a moral imperative to the routines of putting together their packages every night.

The stories are aptly named *packages* because they are a vast array of visuals from different places. Packages, as Postman and Powers (1992) explained, are put together frame by frame, phrase by phrase. There are hundreds of cuts or edits, countless image strung together. During the flood, news packages would sometimes cover a variety of issues or topics, and they were pieced together in a way that moved quickly—that is, quickly enough for TV. Although highly disparate in a sense, the packages were also highly structured. By their own accounts, network correspondents put them together in much the same way they would for any other event. Network routines are established. For local news, however, this was not always the case during the floods.

LOCAL FLOOD NEWS

Local news stations—in Des Moines, Davenport, St. Louis, and Grand Forks—had clearly established routines for newsgathering and reporting in general. Despite previous research findings (Kueneman & Wright, 1975), local broadcast news stations do not necessarily have set policies for dealing with natural disasters, and even if the stations listed did, during the worst of the flooding many of these were necessarily cast aside.

During the height of flood coverage in Grand Forks—the worst weekend in April—individuals started calling WDAZ and asking that reporters broadcast that they had room in their homes for people who had to evacuate. Callers offered their names and telephone number for broadcast. Other individuals called the station crying and asking that reporters broadcast personal messages—that family members or friends call them and let them know they were safe. The station was able to broadcast many of the requests, rendering them literally a community bulletin board—a role they had never played in quite that way before or since. Calls to the station from people in North Dakota, Minnesota, the area of Canada just to the north, and even Michigan moved the staff tremendously. The emotion was evident in news director Mike Brue's voice as he explained what a deep impression that outreach made, and how it made the news team feel such a strong connection to their community and to those who offered to help. He said many of his employees told him that they would never again do anything as important as they did on the news during the flood.

Reporter Terry Dullum conveyed his emotional reaction to the flood when he described how he felt when he realized that the flooding in Grand Forks was rapidly moving north. "I was trying to get the word out," he explained. "I was thinking, my God, the same thing is going to happen to these towns" (referring to those just north and into Winnipeg in Canada). When asked about the emotional reaction of the news team as a whole, he said that people tried to be detached because that is what you are taught, but they were so struck by the hardship.

ABC's Erin Hayes conveyed a personal emotional impact as well when she explained how inspiring it was for her to witness the public service work that WDAZ did for Grand Forks in 1997. As she explained it, half the people who worked at the station lost their homes in the flood, but they were not leaving to check their homes. They were staying on the air 24 hours a day. She said she got goose bumps witnessing what they did. She also said she had never seen a finer public service from a local station.

JOURNALISTIC DUTY AND NATURAL DISASTER

During both floods, a type of journalistic duty was fulfilled by network and local reporters and news staff members, but local reporters had to necessarily go beyond the call of duty because of what they had at stake as individuals and members of an affected community. "It's what we do," Dullum replied when asked about the difficulties of reporting during the flood. He acknowledged, however, that what they did went way beyond journalism. He was referring not only to the emotional impact on the news staff, but also to the fact that they completely altered the news routine.

To keep residents constantly informed, for a number of days the news was broadcast round the clock. In a study of local broadcast gatekeeping during natural disasters, Waxman (1973) found that in a a large-scale disaster, newsgathering and gatekeeping norms are typically abandoned. All information is let through. At WDAZ during the flood, some air time was filled with personal announcements, and some of it was actual raw footage of different areas of the city. Dullum referred to this footage as a *media tour* of the flood. TV cameras propped in boats roamed the silent, flooded streets. Viewers at home were taken on a real-time virtual tour.

Another major break in the routine was that no commercials were broadcast during the local news. Mike Brue explained that when they aired network news and some syndicated programming, they were obligated to run the commercials provided, but during their local broadcast—which was most of the time—they aired only a few PSAs. When asked why, and if they suffered any economic consequences, Brue answered that they did not feel airing commercials would be appropriate, and that, no, there was no negative response from preempted advertisers.

Although the news routines at WDAZ and other local stations were altered during flood coverage, the same could not be said about network coverage. The networks did not offer round-the-clock coverage of either flood, nor would it make sense for them to do so. They did not need to provide raw, live footage to a nationwide audience during either flood. What they offered were edited reports during the regularly scheduled newscasts during the worst days of each flood—the way they report all natural disasters everywhere. The networks reported in a standardized fashion, no doubt with an eye toward economy of time and money and, of course, for ratings. Along those same lines, the networks would not have considered it inappropriate to air commercials during the newscasts that included flood reports, or reports of any other disasters or other instances of human loss, for that matter.

The only indication of a slight break from the usual routine for the networks during the 1993 flood was that anchors Peter Jennings, Tom Brokaw, and Dan Rather, at one point or another, made trips to the midwest to be on the scene for a couple of evening newscasts. Such a move on the part of each network was, no doubt, a ploy for ratings because an anchor on the scene would not necessarily report better than the correspondent already there. Yet an anchor at the site of disaster does give the message to viewers that the situation is dangerous, and gives the impression that the network cares enough to send its top man to oversee. The top anchors at each network are familiar and trusted because they are seen regularly. Sending trusted anchors to the scene of disaster becomes a heroic measure on the part of the anchors and the station. Networks know that this type of virtual news heroics tends to attract viewer admiration and loyalty.

THE ROLE OF TELEVISION NEWS IN NATURAL DISASTER

Some scholars have outlined what they consider appropriate guidelines for news reporters to follow by way of fulfilling their public service duties or ethical obligations during a disaster situation. Graber (1980) wrote that news media have several responsibilities during those times. They should: warn of impending disaster; convey information to officials, relief agencies, and the public; chart the progress of relief and recovery; and dramatize lessons learned to benefit the community in the event of future disaster. Elliot (1989) listed the ethical obligations of news during disaster. He provided a list compiled by the National Research Council's Committee on Disasters and the Mass Media, which is nearly identical to Graber's list. Elliot's suggestions are aimed specifically at reporters. They include: focus on the context of the event, rather than just the body count, and, following the disaster, participate in setting up an agenda for public and government discussions on issues for future disasters. Elliot strongly argued that the press should play a major advocacy role long after disaster strikes.

Can TV news operate both profitably *and* responsibly when covering natural disasters? Are these incompatible goals? Do reporters ever follow the ethical guidelines listed here? Sometimes they do—to a certain degree, but it depends on the disaster, where it happens, and who is covering it. The guidelines for disaster reporting listed earlier do not distinguish types of disasters, nor do they consider the degree to which news staff are affected, either physically or emotionally, as they gather and report information to their audiences. Although the news typically does—perhaps by necessity—standardize coverage of events, reporters, news directors, camera crews, and the like do not always operate from a purely professional stance. Whether they live in the affected zone or fly in to cover the disaster for a few days, to a certain degree they must make a human connection. In her examination of media coverage of the PanAm Flight 103 disaster in Lockerbie, Scotland, Deppa (1994) discussed the ethics involved in reporters approaching grieving victims. Reporters also experience emotional involvement during disasters. Those who work in the capacity of gathering and reporting news have at stake not only their professional reputations and emotional well-being (as well as that of their interview subjects), but also their health and, depending on how close they live to the disaster, the health and safety of their friends and families. In addition, they have at stake the viability of their property and community.

The personal stories recounted here are more than just interesting war stories from reporters who have survived in the trenches of both floods. They point out larger issues regarding natural disaster coverage, some of which have ethical implications. It is clear that local stations in an area hit by a natural disaster are affected differently and have different obligations than do networks who arrive to cover the disaster for an appointed period of time and then leave. There is no ethical dilemma inherent in that situation. However, there were some ethical considerations at stake during the floods on both the local and network levels.

Professionally, the networks did indeed carry out a journalistic duty, to the extent that a nationwide audience received information about the floods. As they see it, the extensive network flood coverage resulted in a literal deluge of aid from viewers nationwide and the attention of the federal government. President Clinton and Vice President Gore made several visits, and sizable amounts of FEMA moneys were earmarked for flood victims both years (Haga, 2001).

Comparing network performance with Graber's and Elliot's lists of news obligations during the flood, it seems Graber's list was partially fulfilled. The networks did inform the public, warn of impending disaster, and dramatize some lessons for future floods. However, they did not fulfill the obligation of public advocate as outlined by Elliot. The three networks tended to focus more on the body count than on the context of the event. More specifically, they emphasized the drama of disaster—looking for the best picture, the most dramatic element, and the best character—and focused on economic and personal losses. They did not put the flood in historical context or spend much time explaining how human efforts over time have contributed to the rivers' tendencies toward flooding (Steinberg, 2000). As public advocates, the networks also fell short. They did not participate in setting an agenda for public and government discussions of disaster issues. Because they proved powerful enough to bring the floods to national attention and help raise federal funds, perhaps they are also ethically obliged to use that power to keep a national conversation going about the reasons for flooding, and the history and context of flooding on the major rivers of the nation. They might also seek to inform about possible long-term solutions.

Regarding network performance behind the scenes at both natural disaster sites, three of the six network correspondents interviewed said that, in flood areas where people lost water, the networks made sure they took care of their own. All three flew in water and, when necessary, food so that the crews could continue to report with minimal discomfort. Although it seems appropriate to take care of the network crew like this, it is important to note that they were, in several instances, given what the people they were reporting on had almost no access to—namely, drinking water and a private, dry place to stay. In some ways, this raises an ethical question similar to that raised when a reporter finds him or herself reporting a wrongdoing or a danger to another person or creature. Do they remain detached and simply report, or do they step in to help? In the case of a natural disaster, is it the responsibility of a network reporter to become involved, or is that an ethical question more relevant to local reporters?

Certainly a special burden is placed on the shoulders of local news stations and staff during natural disaster. This was particularly clear in the case of Grand Forks. Yet are local stations obligated to operate round the clock? Are news workers ethically obliged to stay on the job, risking health, home, and safety? Must stations give up their bread and butter—advertising—in order to offer continuous, uninterrupted coverage? The personal heroics and preempting of commercials at WDAZ run completely counter to what Murrow, Postman, and Powers had to say about TV news. Was WDAZ an anomaly under the circumstances? Should more stations operate that way under circumstances less severe? It seems that reporters and other news staff at local stations, because of their personal and emotional ties to the area, might find it easier to go way beyond the call of journalistic duty during an instance of natural disaster. However, because of the nature of network news, it may be unrealistic to expect the same from on-the-scene correspondents. Could they—and should they—do more than they do right now? Time, resource and commercial considerations will most likely prevent that from happening. Yet ethical questions surrounding all TV coverage of natural disasters must continually be raised.

No doubt the staff of WDAZ in Grand Forks, North Dakota, would agree that they did exactly what they had to do under the circumstances—and would probably do the same again. They fulfilled many of the obligations listed by Graber and Elliot, although it is unclear whether they participated in setting up an agenda for public and government discussion on issues for future disasters.[1] How realistic is it to expect other TV news organizations—network and local—to fulfill these obligations? More importantly, is it even possible for TV to do so on a regular basis? Is that outside the confines of the medium altogether?

---

[1]However, it seems unlikely that they have based on the author's own observations of TV news coverage of Red River flooding in the spring of 2001. The flood coverage of that time was much like flood coverage in 1993 and 1997, with a lot of emphasis on the raging river and little discussion of farming methods and other man-made efforts that contribute to flooding. Certainly there was no discussion of plans made in any year to help alleviate future flooding.

TELEVISION'S ETHICAL LIMITATION

When TV is doing what it does best, as Zettl (1990) claimed happens when it focuses so distinctly on the here and now, and when it offers visual and varied portrayals of a concrete event, does it compromise journalism? More specifically, is it ever possible for TV news to fulfill the litany of ideals some have proposed? Is TV journalistically limited because of its strengths?

The answer to the last question is, "yes." Television is mostly about good pictures and grand effects. It is a mosaic imagery industry, a sensory stimulation machine, an electronic buzz box. The purpose of TV, news included, is to rivet the eye and focus the senses. The value of information on TV, news or entertainment (in many cases they are one and the same), is its ability to retain attention through dramatic video footage, fast-moving image sequences, and the juxtaposition of highly disparate elements. The news frames employed by TV news in covering the flood could not possibly have been the same as those employed by print news despite what some researchers argue. Television news frames stories differently than does print primarily because it is a dramatically different medium. Although it can be said that the underlying theme of Fighting Mother Nature as Garner found in print news was also a major underlying theme in local and national TV news, the quality or meaning of that frame as used on TV is unique. The use of visuals and other elements, and the style of presentation on TV render overall news framing a very different construction. Visualizing the sandbagging efforts, the faces and the postures of those in the battle, and watching, from a moving bird's eye view, the flooded towns and farms—especially when edited together in fast sequence—gives viewers a different understanding of the flood than does reading about these same things in a newspaper or even looking at a still photo.

Moving pictures tend to move people in ways that print does not, but they can leave out a lot of information while offering that much more. Television pictures leave out the details and fill the gap with sensory information that, aesthetically speaking, excites the eye as well as the entire nervous system. As mentioned earlier, one's focus is trained on movement in the moment, on the beautiful and the horrid, not the descriptive and considered. If it is true, as network correspondents Mabrey and Pelle claimed, that politicians and other federal officials made their decisions about how much and what kind of attention to pay the floods based on network TV news coverage, one must consider the implications. If political decision making about how to respond to a natural disaster is based on the visual/aesthetic rhetoric and techniques of TV, it is time to rethink the power of the medium from the perspective of its dire limitations.

Television's limitations as a journalistic medium have as much to do with time and money constraints as with the need to provide constant, changing imagery and effects. The time pressures of TV news work against understanding, coherence, and even meaning, argued Postman and Powers (1992). Both network and local TV news broadcasts are tightly packaged programs. These programs place far less emphasis on what are called *hard news* stories than on soft news or human interest, entertainment-oriented stories. News staff work on tight deadlines. These deadlines and the economic imperative of TV news generally conspire against a thorough examination of issues that have a deep and lasting impact on people's lives. The floods of 1993 and 1997 were events that had broad implications far beyond the flood waters. They were the consequence not only of heavy rainfall and lots of melting snow, but also of a long history of inappropriate building along the river and extensive river control. The only real way in which history was referred to at all in the TV flood stories was by comparing current flooding with floods of the past. The water was at such and such a level during this year; it damaged this many homes, farms, and businesses during that year; and so on. File footage from early floods typically accompanied statistics like these. History was used as a reference to battles of the past.[2]

The constraints that rule TV news as a source of comprehensive natural disaster news also rule out continuous dialogue about natural disaster prevention. Local news may offer more hope here, but the lapse from routine during flood coverage, as illustrated most aptly by WDAZ in Grand Forks and KCCI in Des Moines, seems to be reserved only for instances of dire physical emergency and out of sheer physical necessity. Both local and network news should always report more responsibly on the larger context of natural disasters, including especially the history of such disasters and the ways in which human efforts contribute to their perceived destruction. In the case of the floods, that would mean reporting beyond the Fight With Mother Nature. Although this may not always make for the most dramatic pictures, it will definitely benefit local and national residents who need to understand from both economic and ecological standpoints.

---

[2]During the 2001 spring flooding in Minnesota especially, local TV news made numerous references to the 1997 flooding along the Red River. The references focused most often on water levels and damages during both years.

5

Television, Flood Commemoration, and Popular Culture

"Can't Drown this Town," a TV documentary produced for National Geographic Explorer, aired nationally in 1994. The piece focuses on St. Genevieve, Missouri, a historic French settlement situated just south of St. Louis on the Mississippi River. The town flooded in 1993. The opening shot in the documentary is an aerial shot of the Mississippi shortly after sunrise. Bright rays reflect on a glassy sheen of water. Accompanying that image is a light, melodic, folksy guitar sequence. The mood is nostalgic, "country." The narrator begins: "People who live along the Mississippi mark time by the river. Here some years are landmarks. The touchstones of memory."

At this point, the music shifts from the folksy guitar melody to a deep percussive rhythm. It is a much more menacing sound. The narrator continues: "The flood years. When the waters rise, the people rise up to meet them, often in hand-to-hand combat. But 1993 brought a deluge like none ever before, and the people of the Mississippi found their lives and homes hostage to a foe without mercy or fatigue."

This short introductory sequence includes 11 different images and nine edits. After the first quiet river shot, a montage of flood devastation images follow. They include an Army National Guardsman throwing sandbags off a helicopter, residents and other volunteers furiously sandbagging on the ground, and several shots of the August 1 levee break and farmhouse destruction on the Mississippi River near Columbia, Illinois. All of the images in the introduction contain movement—either swiftly moving water or swiftly moving human bodies. The menacing music continues throughout the entire beginning sequence. Immediately after, the pace slows a bit. The background music is replaced by voices of those who experienced the flood first hand. Flood images continue to fill the screen. One woman comments on the river's power and its will. "The river can take away your home," she explains. Similar voices and sentiments follow. The documentary proceeds with an account of how St. Genevieve successfully fought the river.

The flood documentary described here is only one of many produced shortly after the cresting waters of the 1993 and 1997 floods. Flood specials produced by local stations and networks and other national producers were plentiful after both floods. At least six national retrospectives were produced to commemorate the 1993 or the 1997 flood. These include "Can't Drown This Town," by *National Geographic Explorer*; the 1996 *Nova* documentary, "Flood"; an ABC *American Agenda* piece called "After the Flood"; the CBS *Eye on People* episode called "Flood of 93"; a CBS *Prime Time* special called "Back to the River"; a documentary special produced by the Federal Emergency Management Agency (FEMA) called "The Great Flood of 1993"; and a *Dateline* NBC segment examining the 1997 floods in Fargo and Grand Forks, North Dakota.

On the surface, these nationally produced and televised flood specials focused on re-visiting the flood-torn areas of the midwest and reliving the dramatic deluges of 1993 and 1997. Each one presented image after image of damages, both during and after flooding. Segments were also devoted to the sadness and frustration accompanying clean-up efforts. Most of the specials briefly explored the question of whether flood victims should return to their homes and rebuild, or whether it might be more prudent to move out altogether. Besides these surface intentions, the documentaries and news specials also seemed to be ideal vehicles to showcase the best, most dramatic flood imagery and offer entertainment, perhaps, via the horror and devastation visited on the flooded communities. Certainly the added special effects, including sound, music, and other visual effects, lent a whole new dimension of urgency and drama to each of these national flood specials.

Not only were flood specials produced for national audiences, but many were locally produced and intended for their local broadcast constituencies. Most of the locally produced postflood specials were compilations of flood footage from individual stations. In addition to their day-to-day reports, when the waters had finally subsided, many local stations in particularly flooded areas—Minneapolis/St. Paul, Minnesota; Davenport, Iowa; Hannibal, Missouri/Quincy, Illinois; Des Moines, Iowa; and St. Louis, Missouri—produced special composite videotapes of their best coverage as a way to retell the flood tale.[1] Some of the overt reasons for producing local flood retrospectives were slightly different from the reasons for producing the nationally-aired documentaries and specials. The local stations aired, and then sold, their compilation tapes purportedly to raise funds for flood relief efforts. The local compilation tapes, sold in local retail outlets, were, like their national counterparts, reedited montages presented in narrative format with many added special effects. They were compilations of the most dramatic footage. The local tapes heavily emphasized their own communities and the heroic effort involved in fighting the flood and attempting to bring the community back to normalcy. The tapes were clearly meant to commemorate and historically archive the event, as well as showcase the great footage and efforts of the local news team. It seems the local flood compilation tapes were no less a sensationalized, dramatic presentation of horror and its aftermath than were the national specials.

In addition to the retrospective TV commemorations and documentaries, other kinds of cultural artifacts sprang from these flood events. A partial list includes: songs—flood ballads—written about the flood of 1993; cultural exhibits commissioned and showcased in various local museums; flood aid concerts; an actress and local theater professor's one-woman play about the 1997 Red River flooding in Grand Forks (Ford, 1998); 3 books—mostly photo compilations—published about both floods (Hurley & Hagood, 1993; Malcolm & Strauss, 1996; Hylden & Reuter, 1998); local flood tours; commodities such as T-shirts, postcards, buttons, and even a beer called *Floodweiser* produced and sold in honor of one or both floods; and an annual street dance in Valley Junction, Iowa (part of Des Moines) held each July for several years in remembrance of the 1993 flood. These popular culture artifacts and practices pertaining to flood memory are an indication of the profound

---

[1]An extensive search for local flood specials resulted in compilations put together in 1993 or 1997 by the following stations: KARE 11 TV, Minneapolis, Minnesota; WGEM-TV, Hannibal, Missouri/Quincy, Illinois; WQAD/TV, Davenport, Iowa; KSDK-TV, St. Louis, Missouri; WSIL-TV, Prairie du Rocher, Illinois; WHO-TV, Des Moines, Iowa; KCCI-TV, Des Moines, Iowa; a joint effort by KTCA-TV, KSTP-TV, WCCO-TV, KMSP-TV, KARE-TV, and WFTC-TV in Minneapolis/St. Paul, Minnesota; a joint compilation effort by public TV stations WQPT in Moline, Illinois; KETC in St. Louis, Missouri; Wisconsin Public Television, Iowa Public Television, and KTCA in St. Paul, Minnesota.

impact of flooding on the lives of the individuals and communities involved. The spirit with which they were produced and carried out, as well as the themes, are reminiscent of the postflood TV documentaries.

Television, in fact, has shaped the popular, collective memory of the floods of 1993 and 1997. Television's presentation of the floods as dramatic fights with Mother Nature, its portrayals of victims and heroes, its multiple viewpoints and multisensory stimulation, and its emphasis on the now are evident in the flood commemorations and echoed, in varying degrees, in the rest of the culture that sprang up around the flood. Indeed, TV's technology and aesthetic have shaped flood memories, both on and off screen. This chapter explores TV as popular midwest flood historian and archivist. It also explores the extent to which TV plays a similar role in other natural disasters and what that means.

Because TV is essentially an ephemeral source for information, one's news viewing on any given day is quickly forgotten. Almost as soon as it fades from the screen it fades from memory. News producers, always mindful of tight deadlines, keep their sights on the next news day, the latest update, the breaking event. What aired yesterday is old. The news broadcasts, particularly local ones, do not have a long history of being carefully archived. It was not until 1968 that Vanderbilt University in Nashville, Tennessee, first began to index and archive network broadcast news in a manner similar to the archiving and indexing of print and even film content.[2] The preservation and archiving of local news broadcasts, however, is sporadic at best. Organization and thoroughness varies by station. Some stations retain many of their previous broadcasts, others retain few; those on hand are usually fairly recent.[3] In the case of the 1993 and 1997 midwest floods, local broadcast news teams not only maintained much of their flood footage, at least for a while, but showcased and publicly preserved segments of it in the aftermath.

TELEVISION NEWS, NARRATIVE, AND COLLECTIVE MEMORY

Much has been written about the role of TV in creating a collective or cultural literacy. Noted are particular sitcoms, soap operas, and other

---

[2]The two most complete archives of TV and radio broadcasts are The Museum of Radio and Television located in New York City and The Museum of Radio and Television located in Los Angeles, California.

[3]The author visited five local TV stations 3 years after the 1993 flood to view local flood boadcasts and found that each station had a different system for archiving old broadcasts. Some had a rather extensive archive, whereas other, smaller stations had little beyond 6 months to 1 year previous.

dramas that have reached large audiences. The collective of viewers are said to engage in a ritual activity, gaining and sharing with each other a body of popular cultural knowledge and values. Both James Carey and Josh Meyrowitz discussed in their work the ritual, social maintenance function of TV viewing. The content offers a storehouse of shared knowledge and references while the act of viewing is ritualistic. Television news also performs such a collective function. News watching is perhaps less about information transmission and retrieval than it is about ritual. Watching TV news is habit forming. We tune in to see familiar faces on the screen and to hear them tell us about familiar things in a familiar way. Comfort of familiarity in form and format makes daily viewing pleasurable and entertaining. At the very least, it is also somewhat informative.

During the floods of 1993 and 1997, national and especially local news was no less entertaining, but it became something more. Broadcast news served as the official flood storyteller and, eventually, flood archivist. Documentaries, TV specials, and compilation tapes (hereinafter all are referred to as *flood commemorations*) produced shortly after the waters began to subside indirectly touted themselves as the official flood records. They were meant not only for watching, but for rewatching and remembering into the future. Those who produced them had a vision of their function far beyond raising flood relief funds (in the case of the local commemorations) or providing a one-time entertaining and informative overview. That vision was to record these important events for posterity, a remembrance of the floods' profound impact on many lives—personally, socially, and economically. Producers of the local Des Moines KCCI-TV flood commemoration wrote about their compilation, "The objective of this broadcast was to provide viewers with a videotape that they could keep for many future years as a reminder of how we survived this disaster together."[4] Whether consciously or not, flood commemoration producers were not only archiving the event in video format, but also creating and preserving the images of our collective memory of these floods.

Memory, sociologist Halbwachs (1992) argued, is a collective function. One's memories, he explained, are called to mind through the framework of social memory. In effect, how and what we remember about things and events is a function not of our individual, isolated consciousness, but of shared consciousness. We are directed through the framework of society to remember certain things in a certain way. Halbwachs' theory of collective memory encourages us to understand the powerful social bond that tugs at and binds us together, past, pre-

---

[4]A note about the objective of the flood compilation tape was included as an insert located inside the box in which the flood tape was packaged and sold.

sent, and future. Media scholar Zelizer (1998) used Halbwachs' insight in her analysis of holocaust photos. Photographs, Zelizer explained, are vehicles of collective memory. Although we do not know exactly how photos help us remember, photography is a shared technology, the conventions and use of which are understood, the content of which triggers our memories of the event as captured in still pictures. "We know that collective memories are usable, facilitating cultural, social, economic and political conventions, establishing solidarity and continuity" (p. 4), Zelizer argues. She explains that photographs solidify the social order because they tend to turn into iconic representations that stand for belief systems, themes, and epochs. The photographic image helps stabilize collective memory's fluctuating nature. Images in film and on TV do the same. Television images of the floods were captured first as daily news items, but then select shots and video sequences became iconic representations of the impact and implications of the entire disaster in all its construed intensity and violence.

In the flood commemorations, select shots and sequences were edited together to create a narrative unique to each production. The flood narrative that unfolded in a particular commemoration tape depended partly on the kind of story each production team wished to tell. Both overt and underlying themes were evident in all of them. News in general tends to be narrative in structure, explained Bird and Dardenne (1988). They argued that journalists draw on storytelling patterns because such patterns give people a necessary schema for understanding the world. It is important to examine the ways in which news operates narratively—that is, in the ways familiar stories are played out over and over again, in the kinds of dramatic characters portrayed, and in the dramatic arc of a given storyline. Popular culture, and particularly mass media, are the current sources of folklore, argued historian Levine (1992). Bird (1996) wrote about news as narrative and as folklore. She used as an example a story, widely reported in the mid-1980s, of an HIV-positive woman who was supposedly spreading the AIDS virus by having anonymous sex with men she met in Dallas nightclubs. This story, Bird argued, was an example of news as folklore because, although the story could not be verified, it rang true at that time because it addressed a growing collective anxiety about AIDS transmission through heterosexual sex. The story put a specific narrative frame around a collective anxiety in an attempt to make sense of it. The story quickly caught on in the Dallas metropolitan area and beyond. It was, in fact, a narrative that deeply resonated with a national audience.

Local and national flood commemoration tapes showcase news as narrative, folklore, and archive of collective memory. The narrative thread that emerges in most daily ongoing broadcast news stories is not always a conscious choice on the part of journalists, although it is often the structure within which they present the facts. In the flood commemorations, however, narrative structure is a foreground element—a clearly conscious choice. Select daily news items have been repackaged and narratively streamlined. Each is structured as a grand narrative of loss and survival—a tale about a flood that turned a quiet city, small town, and/or rural area into chaos. Themes that emerge within the grand narrative include a host of heroic efforts by the community, the idea of solidarity, us against the rivers, and finally of victory of some sort over Mother Nature. It is man versus nature, the underdogs and the helpless versus the awesome and unexplainable. A subtler message in these specials is that the news team/station, also affected by the flooding, heroically came through for the community—the videotaped commemoration as clear evidence. Each tape features a narrator or team of narrators and includes specially selected music and other sound and visual effects that enhance the preselected footage and support the grand narrative. The end result is a visual keepsake, a dramatic construction, a marker of collective memory.

LOCAL FLOOD COMMEMORATIONS

All of the tapes were produced in a similar fashion. They begin with a swiftly paced montage of images of heavy flooding or related destruction, human emotion, emergency action, and overall chaos. The sense of urgency constructed at the beginning is a compressed version of what unfolds throughout the video. Dramatic music is laid under the initial montage to reinforce urgency. Visual and sound effects help create the melodramatic tone. Introductory montage segues into the narrator's introduction. The narrator or team of narrators is either the station's top anchor(s) or top field reporter(s). It is a familiar and trusted face on the screen. The narrator gives background information and a quick summary of the disaster, the community efforts, and so on. Following that segment is a chronological series of dramatic, touching, frightening, and uplifting segments. Each focuses on a different compelling aspect of the flood—from the way it began, to rising tension within the community as flood waters continued to rise, to emergency levee repairs and endless sandbagging, to major destruction, to pleas for federal aid, to presidential or other official visits, to evacuation by National Guardsman, to relief from the Red Cross, to emotional turmoil in the wake of major losses, and, typically, to a sentimental recap of events and a look toward the future. Each tape includes its individual tales of supreme heroics and devastating loss, but overall the videotapes all paint a similar picture:

fighting nature, overcoming loss, community solidarity, and looking with hope toward the future. Scenes with the narrator(s) who aids in the overall comprehension of the tape and reinforces the message of loss, survival, and heroism punctuate the segments.

KCCI, channel 8, the CBS affiliate in Des Moines, Iowa, produced "Flood of '93," an hour-long commemoration that looks back at the flood from the perspectives of its own news staff members. The entire introductory sequence of this commemoration tape, a rather lengthy 2 minutes, includes 47 different images and many different kinds of added sound: thunder, synthesized music, percussion, overlapping reporter voices, and other overlapping voices culled from previous newscasts. The highly stylized audiovisual sequence features editing and effects to match sound and image. Some of the images are slowed down for added emotional and visual impact; others are speeded up to match the staccato bass rhythm in the last few measures of the musical piece produced exclusively for this tape. The tone is set. There is urgency, destruction, and fighting against the forces of nature. It is not unlike a trailer for an upcoming action-adventure film.

The first visual in the introductory sequence is rain falling, followed quickly by lightening and the sound of thunder. At this point, the synthesized music begins—percussion and keyboard—and the image montage speeds up. One after another we see images of people running, people sandbagging, the Army National Guard working to evacuate areas and save people, the water rushing. One image is an extreme closeup of a woman crying. A slow-motion image near the end of the montage is of Army National Guardsmen running with tree branches, although it is not clear where they are going. The visual feast ends as the music ends—abruptly.

Then the narrator, anchor Kevin Cooney, appears in midshot, standing in a studio. He introduces the tape.

> The sight, the sound, the images that are etched in the minds and hearts of all of us who were a part of the flood of '93. Hi, I'm Kevin Cooney. As a reporter and anchor for TV8, I've covered many stories that touched and changed the lives of Iowans, but I don't think that any of them can compare with the stories of courage, love, help and survival that unfolded day after day in the flood of '93.

The rest of the commemoration includes about nine different segments, each focused on a different aspect of the flood. The segments are presented in rough chronological sequence. It all begins on July 8. The worst of the flooding in Des Moines unfolded during the month of July, and the commemorative tape gives a day-by-day account, a major part of which includes about 2 weeks when the city was without drinking water because of contamination in the treatment plant. First the tape covers the sheer amount of rainfall experienced in the area in that spring and early summer. Subsequent sections cover the rescue by Guardsmen and volunteers, President Clinton's visit, the death of one fireman in a rescue attempt, clean-up efforts, the loss of water, a music video about flood heroes and victims, and finally the birth of one staff member's son right in the midst of the flooding.

Several segments stand out as particularly good examples of how images and effects reinforced the grand narrative and its supporting themes. One segment recalls a specific evening in early July, one of the worst nights for the area. "Des Moines looked like a war zone that night," recalls Cooney in voice-over. Accompanying images include National Guardsmen in fatigues and military jeeps, sandbagging from a helicopter, fixing a levee, and generally taking charge of and rescuing an area hurling out of control by the raging Des Moines and Raccoon Rivers, both of which converge in downtown Des Moines. Production techniques that enhance the military tone of this segment include the action music laid under, fast cuts, use of strobe editing, and some slow motion shots of Guardsmen at work in any number of capacities. Techniques such as these succeed in expanding the drama to its fullest.

Another particularly dramatic segment is the music video inserted more than halfway into the tape. The song "Unexpected Friends" by Sandi Patti is a slow ballad with a love song feel. That song is accompanied by an entire sequence of slow motion shots, heavy on the close-ups, of people working hard to save sections of the city and surrounding area from the flood. Smiling faces, tired faces, sad faces, and determined faces appear one right after another in this section. There are volunteers, farmers, very young people, elderly people, and people literally leaning on each other for comfort. This is the tear-jerker segment. The music combined with images and the technique of slow motion successfully pull out all the emotional stops. The point is solidarity, community, *us* against *it*.

The final full segment in the piece is about the birth of baby Lucas to one of the KCCI photographers. In this section, narrator Kevin Cooney speaks off camera directly to the newborn, whom we see in several still shots, about the worst days of flooding in the city, and about the coincidence of his birth in the midst of flood chaos. Almost all of the shots in this sequence are slow motion as well. The *life* metaphor is used to parallel Lucas' new one and the city's newfound one. Both made it safely to the other side. Accompanying the images and narration is a soft, soothing melody.

Finally, we come back to Cooney in the studio. He raises a glass of water to the camera as he says, "Thank you [the community] for helping us [the station] get through the greatest disaster in our history." The credits roll and the soft melody continues just below.

Throughout this piece, reporters, photographers, editors, and other staff members from the station discuss what was happening in the city and especially how that affected their ability to cover the flooding. News staff were interviewed inside the station—usually shot in medium to medium close up—about their personal experiences and feelings as they covered the flood. Some were quite emotional, others were more matter-of-fact as they described the rigors of flood coverage during that worst period. Interspersed with these interview sequences were each of the segments described earlier, and countless images taken from the video storehouse of daily flood footage the station had previously aired.

The KCCI flood commemoration included no historic information. Produced in late 1993, it focused exclusively on one flood and the efforts of this one station to bring it to the audience. There was nothing about whether there had been flooding in the past nor about the flood walls and other flood-protection devices built around the two converging rivers to keep the city and surrounding areas dry. Printed on an insert that accompanied the videotape was a concise explanation of the purpose of the broadcast as the station wished to present it. The insert reads:

> This broadcast was a compilation of the multi-faceted effort by KCCI-TV to serve its community during its worst natural disaster in history, the Great Flood of 1993. . . .
>
> The goal of our coverage and this broadcast was to provide vital, life-saving information to the residents of our community. KCCI-TV suspended normal programming for five straight days to provide the pictures and the information the public needed to survive.
>
> The objective of his broadcast was to provide viewers with a videotape that they could keep for many future years as a reminder of how we survived this disaster together. . . .

The tape was produced to raise flood relief funds and serve as a public relations vehicle for the station. Clearly, the station also intended for it to be the quintessential local flood archive. Such was the case with all of the local flood commemoration tapes. The nationally produced tapes differ in some ways, but in the final analysis are not that different.

NATIONAL FLOOD COMMEMORATIONS

The *Nova* special, "Flood," was produced and aired in 1996, a few years after the 1993 flood, but it is about that flood. The introductory montage sequence lasts 2 minutes and 30 seconds and contains 30 different flood images. At the very beginning, after a short string of flood images, the narrator begins: "Unfolding in slow motion, a flood is unlike any other natural disaster." At this point the electronic, pounding bass of the music begins. The narrator continues: "The River's caretakers, the Army Corps of Engineers, are thrust into a state of emergency."

Here we see footage of a meeting room cramped with middle-aged White men who obviously work for the Army Corps. We listen to a few concerned sound bites as they discuss the next appropriate course of action. The music continues. Next we see video footage of Army Jeeps filled with men in fatigues. We see them sandbagging. The narrator returns: "By mid-July National Guard units from across the country are sent to help in what is becoming an all-out war against nature."

The music intensifies, it pounds more heavily. Images of sand-baggers and soldiers are strung together; the pace of editing intensifies: "By August 1st, the river appears unstoppable."

Here are scenes from the levee breach outside Columbia, Illinois, and the famous farmhouse destruction shots. Yet this commemorative tape includes footage of other farms and farmhouses taken down in that breach, not the original August 1 shot seen so often on network coverage and in other commemorations.

"Tens of thousands of residents are forced from their homes. Livestock scramble for high ground. And some people narrowly escape with their lives."

The music slows somewhat and grows quieter. Accompanying these words and music are images of farms and a herd of pigs trying to stay atop a barn roof as they attempt to remain above the rising water. We see a shot of a mother wading through waist-high water while carrying her young child. We also see vehicles attempting to drive through the rising water to the safety of dry land—trying desperately to stay above the rising water.

Now the music has become more melodic, although the pictures are ever-more devastating.

"Uprooting entire communities. Destroying property. Disrupting life over a nine-state area. This was the most costly flood in U.S. recorded history."

With these last words, the camera offers a broad panorama of a flooded farm area as taken from inside a helicopter. From here we can scan to the horizon. The camera moves in the helicopter almost 180 degree and rests, finally, on a white farmhouse jutting sideways out of about 10 feet of flood water. The water had moved it off its foundation, then resettled it at an angle. The camera rests on that image as the introductory sequence comes to a close.

The subsequent segments of the *Nova* commemorative documentary follow the flooding as it heads south along the Mississippi River during the summer of 1993. This commemoration differs from other local and national commemorations. Although the pictures are no less dramatic, the narrative is less urgent in tone, less hyperbolic. Because the documentary was produced several years after the flood, the interview subjects, including flood victims, are more reflective about their experience. They are not still in the throes of disaster and clean-up.

After the dramatic introduction, a significant portion of the 1-hour documentary explores the reasons for flooding along the river, the history of human intervention, historic federal government bail-outs, and why people continue to live in the once natural flood plains along the Mississippi. Interviews with several officials focus on these issues. A representative of an organization called American Rivers,[5] representatives of the Army Corps of Engineers, a government representative in St. Charles County, Missouri, who buys out flood victims, and an agricultural specialist who studies the effect of farming on flood plains and talks on camera about various types of human intervention on the river. Each raises questions about the wisdom of populating what were once areas that served as Mississippi wetlands, holding water for the river as it regularly flowed over in an attempt to rejuvenate itself.

However, the images and music are every bit as dramatic as they are in other commemorations. A clear contradiction exists in the piece. Two threads run parallel. They are the dichotomous neutral river/bad river. Most of the verbal subject matter tends toward reflective consideration of why the water floods and what that means for people living in its flood zone. Yet the Fight With Mother Nature theme is also evident. Some of the words, many of the pictures, as well as the music tend toward portraying the river with a will of its own, bent on bringing harm to people, in need of control, and, basically, in the wrong for causing what it caused people during that summer.

The introductory sequence sets up the bad river thread for the documentary, particularly in its use of the battle metaphor as the narrator describes an "all-out war with nature." The images of National Guardsmen and the menacing, pounding music initially set the tone of

---

[5]American Rivers, located in Washington, DC, is a nonprofit organization dedicated to protecting and restoring America's river systems. It publishes an annual report of activities and other reports on the ecological viability of river systems throughout the United States.

river gone wrong. Original footage, taken from local and national news, of sandbaggers, of the faces of people in the midst of the disaster, of working together against the odds, all reinforce the bad river scenario. These images portray the people as protagonist and river as clear antagonist. Several interview subjects belie a neutral, reflective demeanor, focusing instead on people's own lack of control over it and other larger forces. One Army Corps spokesperson, recounting the intensity and anxiety of trying to keep propane gas tanks afloat in South St. Louis, describes the relief of the downstream levee break on August 1 which meant they no longer had to worry about a massive explosion. "God decided we had enough," he said. Likewise, a district levee commissioner from rural Illinois explains his thoughts at the time when the levee he thought would break did not. "I think we've been visited with a miracle," he recalls thinking. Finally, Army Corps spokesperson Dave Mueller, featured in several sections of the piece, describes with great emotion, sometimes choking back tears, how difficult it was for him to witness the Columbia, Illinois, levee break on August 1, after working so hard with the people in the area to maintain its strength in the hope that it would remain steadfast.

The musical score, mostly an electronic pulse that fluctuates only slightly throughout the documentary, helps retain the dramatic continuum even at those times when the subject matter is neutral or historically reflective. The musical fluctuations coincide with the information presented in any given segment. Yet there are no other added sound effects beyond the music. Editing techniques in the *Nova* piece are not spectacular as they are in many other commemorations. There is no use of slow motion, no strobe, no wild fluctuations in the pacing. The quieter demeanor of the style coincides with the neutral river thread in the documentary.

Reinforcing the neutral river idea, besides the informative talking head interviews with the spokespersons mentioned earlier, is the emphasis on the history of river intervention. *Flood* focuses on historic human intervention in two different sections. In the first, near the beginning, we see archive film footage of intense Army Corps of Engineers intervention along the Mississippi in the early 1930s. At that time, the Corps built countless levees and lock and dam systems, from Minneapolis/St. Paul south to St. Louis. This effort followed the famous flood of 1927, which had a devastating effect on the people who had settled along the upper Mississippi River (Barry, 1997). The second historic segment included original footage from Pare Lorentz's famous film documentary, "The River," produced in 1938 and commissioned by the U.S. federal government's Resettlement Administration. That documentary celebrated efforts to control the Mississippi River and other American rivers through the progressive efforts of those interested in capturing its potential for economic growth.[6]

Despite all of the information presented on human intervention and the river's historic overflowing to accommodate its own ecological needs, this flood commemoration persists in retaining the bad river thread, mostly via the themes of fighting Mother Nature and community solidarity. A segment on saving Prairie du Rocher, Illinois, by manually breaching a nearby levee to relieve water pressure highlights how hard the citizens of that town worked together in an effort to preserve their homes and some of their farmland. Near the end of the documentary, the images of farm flooding, the destruction of homes, and the sad and weary faces of those who lost in the flood and those who will not move away from the river are presented with soft melodic music. We are compelled to feel pain and their loss, to side with them, and to cheer on their efforts to continually fight the river. The piece ends with the white farmhouse jutting sideways out of the water. It pauses there just a moment. The heartland, it suggests, will reemerge.

An important element of the commemoration tapes that cannot be left unexamined is the fact that all of them, to varying degrees, emphasize the struggles and heroics of the news. KCCI-TV in Des Moines was particularly blatant in its self-focus. The KCCI videotape emphasizes how the Des Moines news staff struggled to stay on the air during the worst part of the flooding (and indeed that part is true and must be included) to bring necessary information to the public. The entire videotape is a series of stories about the personal experiences of the anchors and reporters at the station, mostly told in first person.

The station's heroism is portrayed as both mythic and highly sentimental. All of the commemorative tapes, not just KCCI's, include an element of TV news heroism. To do otherwise would be to miss a golden public relations opportunity. Because the tapes are meant to be viewed for years to come, and because the profits from the sales of the tapes purportedly went toward flood relief, the good name of the local news will be preserved in the community's own cultural history.

The fact that TV news is a profit-making venture raises questions about its capability as community archivist. Television news has a commercial agenda, and gatekeeping choices made in daily news reports reflect that agenda—hence the dramatic sensationalism and what is often critiqued as excess violence. In the case of the flood com-

---

[6]Pare Loretz's "The River" deals with technological progress in a rather positive way. It details the mechanization and technological developments used by the Tennessee Valley Authority, under federal government authority, to *tame* the Missippippi and other rivers to be more economically viable resources. For more information, see http://xroads.virginia.edu/~1930s/film/lorentz/river.html.

memoration tapes, local television news stands to profit in several ways. Profits from tape sales were to go to flood relief efforts, often to the Red Cross. Yet whether that happened is worth questioning. Pete Barrett, news director at KMOV-TV in St. Louis, Missouri, revealed that KMOV produced a flood special and sold the tapes to local residents to raise flood relief funds but the profits really went to pay off the exorbitantly high bill for helicopter rental the station had racked up during the 1993 flood (personal communication, July 9, 1996). Certainly this station's alleged deed could be the exception. Perhaps the profits from other tape sales really did go to relief efforts. Whether they did or did not is secondary to the larger implications of commercial TV operating as archivist for the collective memory of a history-making local event.

The bulk of news profits come from advertisers that pay for time based on the news show's ratings. That is the case no matter what the event covered. An eye toward profits leads to reporting that is partial, with emphasis often on the dramatic and sensational. It also leads to deemphasis or diversion in others. In the case of the floods, both heightened drama and deemphasis were part of the local day-to-day reporting. This was first-level gatekeeping with profits in mind. When the daily reports were reedited into local and national flood commemoratives, second-level gatekeeping occurred, and the flood stories were even more streamlined. Add to that a focus, in each tape, on the local station's own heroic efforts and the flood story becomes even more a victim of commercial considerations. The stories of the two floods, based on the accounts in these commemorations, are not historically accurate renditions to say the least. Certainly revisionist history is not unique to these commemoratives, to TV or even to print media. But when stories are enhanced to the extent that they are in these tapes—thanks to special effects and astounding editing techniques—and when they are commercialized as they are, one cannot help but both marvel and shudder. With amazement, we can consider the resulting collective memory of these floods and the extent to which it will manifest in future public policies regarding use of land, water, and other resources.

FLOOD COMMEMORATIONS, COLLECTIVE MEMORY AND FOLKLORE

Their money-making potential duly noted, on the cultural level, the flood commemorations are also examples of news as narrative and news turned folklore on the way to establishing itself in the collective memory. To make sense of the chaos wrought by unprecedented flooding, huge economic damages, and emotional turmoil, TV news used a familiar narrative structure—the tale of unified struggle against a formidable force—to help make sense of a dire human predicament. Day-to-day news reports reflected that structure, albeit in disjointed manner, but the local and national commemorations clearly unified the narrative. The local flood commemorations, the most dramatic of the local news footage plus stylized editing and effects, almost completely exclude footage that does not fit the version of the flood story that makes it mythical. At the local stations, there were a number of daily news reports that discussed that problems with flooding on the Mississippi River, for one, is in many ways a direct result of over 100 years of human tampering. In the later commemorations, the flooding is present-ed as if it were a mystery, a call from Mother Nature or God, and that floods are an angry lashing out, a warning, or even a punishment. Also missing is news footage indicating that in many local areas—in St. Louis and Davenport, particularly—neighborhood evacuations by local emer-gency squads, police, and the National Guard was not always an easy or pleasant task. In fact, many residents who were required to leave their homes were furious. There were daily reports of struggles with authori-ties, mostly in poorer neighborhoods, where residents not given com-plete information and were not always treated with respect. Heated arguments and other such struggles were erased in the flood commemo-rations. Included instead was only footage that showed the communities working together as a team to overcome nature's wrath. Most of the national commemorations were the same, particularly *National Geographic*'s "Can't Drown This Town" and the CBS *Eye on People* flood special. *Nova*'s "Flood" did explore the human causes of river flooding, but the sounds and images that ultimately encourage identifying the river as a raging and unpredictable antagonist overshadow its consid-ered and historic approach.

In the narrative structure of journalism, the flood events retain a mythic quality. The metaphysical aura surrounding the flood and why it happened, the unlimited strength and endurance exhibited by local resi-dents, and the nearly complete harmony in which the communities worked are the stuff of a superb drama for the local and national histori-cal archives—fit commemorations for generations to come. Journalism exerts what Zelizer (1992) called its cultural authority when it identifies the flood in such dramatic terms, thus preserving it as such for years to come. Yet it is not the practice of journalism generally that identified the flood as it did. It is TV journalism specifically that has created the floods that we hold in our collective memory.

The flood commemoration tapes are mythic folklore specifically because of the way images, words, and sounds depict how the flooding came about and how local communities and the nation responded. The tapes are a highly structured narrative response to collective anxieties about nature in general and the rivers in particular. Underlying the original news footage, and intensified in the commemorative tapes, is an intense fear. Yet is it fear of nature, or fear of how we have responded, and may very well continue to respond, where nature is concerned? Ultimately it may be fear of our own collective inability to foresee where human efforts to control and overcome nature as set apart from us eventually leads. Television is a fit medium to play out those fears while also diverting them. Because images and sounds can freely play with and alter the course of an event in representation, certainly it is feasible that they can also divert our attention. In the case of the 1993 and 1997 floods, TV news throws the blame back on nature, reinforcing nature as a separate entity and allowing us to continue shifting the blame while celebrating our own heroism in our fight against nature.

POPULAR CULTURE OF THE FLOODS

The fear and heroism—and profiteering—identified with television flood commemorations are at the core of numerous other popular culture events and artifacts spawned by the flooding. The collective memory of the floods are retained in these as well, but in a deep sense they pay homage to TV's initial identification of the flood events as ultimately a spectacular fight with Mother Nature.

 Heroism and solidarity, above all else, reign supreme in flood popular culture. Hatfield and McCoy, two popular radio personalities on KJJY Radio in Des Moines, in 1993 wrote a flood ballad called "Can't Drink the Water." It is a light-hearted country folk song about water loss in Des Moines. It makes light of what was, for the residents of Des Moines, a grueling situation and celebrates their collective ability to get through the hardship. Flood Aid concerts, featuring the likes of John Mellencamp and Willie Nelson were scheduled in Des Moines, Davenport, and St. Louis to raise money for flood victims. Some of them had to be canceled because of continued flood dangers; others ran as scheduled. Like the farm aid concerts of the 1980s, the flood aid concerts stressed the hardships of the good people of the midwest who were faced with a dire situation. In the 1980s the enemy was bankers and others forcing farmers to foreclose on family farms and lose the land their families had worked for so long. In 1993, the enemy was the river forcing farmers to lose those lands. Music and musicians celebrated and sang about the ability to fight back and win.

 As waters began to subside, flood tours, t-shirts, buttons, postcards, a beer called *Floodweiser* (brewed for a time in the Grand Forks,

North Dakota, area), and other commodities and memorabilia were available to local residents. Enterprising business people quickly saw the potential to make a buck by capitalizing on the situation. Flood tours took residents and outside tourists to the same places they had seen on the TV screen. For a few dollars, one got a first-hand view of water damages. People could also buy t-shirts and buttons with slogans that identified them as flood survivors, flood fighters, sandbaggers, and the like. These were meant to be light-hearted commemorations, but they also filled a need for people to outwardly signify themselves as part of the flood fight. Purchasing a T-shirt or button allowed them to identify with a group of like fighters/survivors.

The annual flood festival and the one-woman show "Flood of Memories" are examples of dramatic displays or practices highlighting the human struggles and celebration of solidarity following the floods of 1993 and 1997. For several years after the 1993 flood, Valley Junction, in West Des Moines, Iowa, included on its events calendar each July the annual flood festival. The festival is slated to return on the 10th anniversary of that flood. The 1-day festival featured a street dance where people would come together and celebrate their ability to fight and win against the river. With music, dance, and celebration in general, it was a remembrance of what local residents and merchants had endured and presumably conquered. Valley Junction is a low-lying area near the Raccoon River. No one—business owner or home owner—moved out after the flood. As long as they stay dry, presumably, they will continue to celebrate each year. Playwright and actress Frances Ford's one-woman show, "Flood of Memories," recounts the flood of 1997 which engulfed most all of Grand Forks, North Dakota (personal communication, April 20, 2001). The performance features over a dozen characters, each a composite of actual local residents who told their own personal stories about their flood experience. The stories became part of an oral history project sponsored by the North Dakota Museum of Art. Ford took the stories and constructed a play that she performed at the Museum and in Canada. The stories woven together in this drama focus on how people struggled as individuals and with each other against the water when it ran high and even long after it subsided. A good deal of the narrative also includes the themes of community and solidarity and, finally, of celebration of what they endured. Ultimately the play—like the street dance and other locally produced and consumed commodities and exhibits about the floods—reifies the culture versus nature dichotomy. Nature, something to be awed by and afraid of, is a force to be fought against when it gets too close, when it oversteps its bounds.

Even the Internet kept people informed of the floods as it encouraged the fight/solidarity/heroism triad. The "Fargo Flood" homepage was launched shortly after the start of flooding by North Dakota State University in Fargo, North Dakota. A link from the NDSU homepage, the Fargo Flood homepage is still regularly updated and includes information on current river levels, emergency management, information on flood clean-up, National Weather Service information, and flooding history, among other links (www.ndsu.nodak.edu/fargoflood). The University of Manitoba launched and maintains a similar site for residents of that area who were also affected by the flooding Red River in 1997 (www.manitoba.ca/news/flood97). While providing useful, up-to-date information for local residents and others interested in river levels in those areas, the Web sites also feature spectacular flood images, not unlike those available in flood commemoration photo books published after the floods of '93 and '97 and on television. The images depict incredibly high flood levels; furious sandbagging efforts; forlorn, determined and exuberant faces; and many other emotionally riveting shots. Unlike TV, the Web sites allow interested parties to access flooding information and related links at all times. Like TV, they tout themselves as electronic flood archives. Like TV, they offer an electronic, multifaceted, and highly visual means of remembering, reliving, and retaining the disasters.

TELEVISION AS NATURAL DISASTER ARCHIVE

How useful a medium is TV as a natural disaster archive? As a repository—and shaper—of collective memory? Given its strengths and weaknesses as a communication medium, one must seriously consider its viability as creator and keeper of significant events that involve the natural world.

It is interesting that the 1993 flood, and to a lesser degree the 1997 flood, merited the number of TV commemorations they did. No other natural disaster of recent memory has been so commemorated, particularly by local news stations. Perhaps because of the sheer amount of human damages sustained, the breadth of that damage, and the longevity of the floods in general, the flood events took on a significance other national disasters such as hurricanes and tornadoes have not. Although storms such as these are named, they are not commemorated to the same degree as the floods have been. Yet TV certainly does pay some attention to these natural disasters.

Because TV is unique in its capacity for event construction, to assess it as a means to shape natural disaster memory, one must look again at its strengths and weaknesses, particularly with regard to natural disaster representation. One way to do so is to look at other kinds of natural disaster accounts on TV, both fictional and non-fiction. Following is a discussion of other popular televised natural disaster programs. The discussion is framed in terms of TV's key characteristics: capacity for multiple viewpoints, visual bias, penchant for drama, and overall commercial imperative. All of these are notably at play across a wide spectrum of televised natural disaster programs. It becomes clear, when examining the range of TV natural disaster accounts, that similar themes emerge. Because of television's production techniques and content requirements, many disasters tend to look alike.

Since the mid- to late-1990s, natural disasters have received ample TV time on both broadcast and cable networks. Natural disasters and their victims have been reported on, commemorated, and dramatized in daily news reports, special documentary features, and even in made-for-TV movies. A sample of recent fare includes a 1999 NBC news piece on flooding in North Carolina; a Weather Channel documentary special called, "Five Great Disasters," which looks back at Hurricane Hazel, a tornado in Pennsylvania, a flash flood on the Big Thompson River in the western Rocky Mountains, a blizzard in Vermont and a look back at the Dust Bowl of the 1930s; a History Channel week-long "Nature's Fury" series on its program, *The 20th Century*, hosted by Mike Wallace, which devoted entire evenings each to earthquakes, firestorms, hurricanes, and tornadoes; and finally, a made-for-TV-movie on the Fox network called *Tornado*. All of these are televised remembrances and renditions of natural disasters that have occurred in the United States during the 20th century. Each is a typical example of natural disaster presentation on television, and all of them, in different ways and to different degrees, showcase television's ability to create a uniquely dramatic event wherein humans were unpredictably victimized by powerful natural forces. Whether they all have a similar impact on their audience is not known. Media critic Lippert (1993), writing in *Mediaweek*, argued that a plethora of made for TV movies about disasters—*Triumph of Disaster: The Hurricane Andrew Story*, for example—actually confirm for most people that the disaster has indeed occurred. Whether dramatic fictional accounts more powerfully confirm or convey a natural disaster than non-fiction or documentary accounts is not known. What is known is that TV's characteristic strength is the creation of a sensational event.

Television's multiple viewpoints are created through production techniques such as camera work, editing, pacing and added special effects, both visual and aural. In the specific ways they were employed to commemorate these disasters, the documentaries on the Weather Channel and the History Channel resemble the flood specials examined earlier. The way the disasters are described and presented on the small screen in these documentary specials entails the editing together of previous disparate footage—the most dramatic and the most enticing—in such a way as to portray many different facets of each. News footage, along with other types of video coverage of a disaster, is edited into organized sequences, some of which are fast and some slowed down considerably to draw out select aspects of each event. Music, sound effects, and other visual techniques regulate the overall feel of the individual segments and the pieces as a whole. The result is that each individual natural disaster has a TV look that resembles all the others. The documentaries cover a wide range of economic, emotional, and social issues surrounding each disaster. So it was with the 1993 and 1997 flood commemorations. As in the flood commemorations, the multiple viewpoints presented in the natural disaster documentaries leave out the critical historical examination of human efforts that have impeded the natural environment, with the result of encouraging a human economic toll because of regular natural occurrences.

The visual renditions of the natural disaster programs are compelling and quite dramatic. NBC includes a segment in one of its fall 1999 nightly newscasts on flooding in Princeville, North Carolina, an area built on flood-prone bottom land, as reporter Bob Dotson explains. The segment does not feature helicopter shots as did the midwest flood news, but includes many shots of homes barely standing in almost 10 feet of water and homes, after the flooding, completely in ruins. These shots are edited together with close-up shots of the faces of several Princeville residents who have lost almost everything. The extreme close-ups are reserved for the teary faces of several women who described what they have lost. Shots like these are typical for news of disaster. The visuals cut back and forth between long shots of destruction and close shots of emotion. A slightly different way of visually portraying the devastating effects of nature can be found in the Fox made-for-TV-movie, *Tornado*. It is shot like a horror film. The movie begins with exterior shots of flat, almost barren, rural Adrian, Texas, located in that part of the state referred to as *tornado alley*, or so we read on the screen. The camera , which pans the rural terrain, rests a moment on the outside of a modified ranch-style middle-class house. The film cuts to the interior of the home, where we see a typical domestic scene. A mother and her two daughters are at the kitchen sink and kitchen table, respectively, happily absorbed in their activities. Suddenly the sky darkens and the window shatters, both out of nowhere. A frightened mother and her two children scream and then run in a panic down the basement stairs as if being chased by an evil monster. They huddle close and cling to each other as the storm proceeds to rock and shake the house. Finally, the shaking and wind stop. Cut to an exterior shot of a house almost flattened on the still, barren plain. The visuals in this fictional TV movie are more obviously heightened reality than the news visuals, but both are clearly heightened drama.

The words, in all of the televised natural disasters examined here, also tend toward the dramatic, specifically to verbalize the familiar drama of humans versus nature. A dramatic subtheme is the unpredictability of nature coupled with its wrath. Images, words, and music worked together to intensify the chaos whipped up by nature. In the NBC news piece reporter Bob Dotson explains that historic Princeville, North Carolina, was the first chartered community for free slaves. At the end of the piece, he closes by explaining that, "A place forged out of war and slavery finds its strength in hard times." The words suggest that the residents of Princeville are not strangers to struggle, but now their struggle is with the forces of nature. On the Weather Channel documentary, the narrator explains at the beginning that, "The threat of disaster hangs over our lives." He goes on to say that, "The element of surprise is disaster's most important weapon." Mike Wallace sums it up best in the program about tornadoes in the 20th century's "fury week" series when he explains at the beginning of the program that tornadoes are "perverse, unpredictable, and for those caught in their path, they can be their worst nightmare." At the beginning of the Fox film "Tornado," words of warning scroll up the screen: "Scientists warn that due to the increase in global warming, existing weather patterns are becoming steadily more severe; causing . . . stronger hurricanes . . . worse floods . . . longer droughts . . . and devastating tornadoes."

All of these natural disaster programs highlight the chaos wrought by nature as foe. On the Internet, one also has access to natural disaster drama. At the *Discovery.com* Web site, maintained by cable TV's Discovery Channel, one can find out more about the channel's featured disaster documentaries such as *Earthquake*, *Volcano*, and *Hyper Hurricanes*. The Weather Channel also features and sells a "Nature's Fury" video set, which includes individual programs such as *Lightning*, *Hurricane*, and *Killer Quake*. The Weather Channel also sells, through a small catalog, CD-ROMs and other videos about extreme weather. The framework for understanding nature is the same in all of these electronic presentations. Mother Nature runs afoul, and we are merely pawns of the unpredictable forces that surround us. The drama is heightened by the sense of unpredictability and power emphasized over and over again. These TV fictions and nonfictions play on our fears of nature, which, as argued earlier, may be displaced fears of ourselves, and specifically fear of our own ignorance and/or unwillingness to take a close look at the fruits of progress as they impact the land and surrounding environment.

Television only encourages us to continue looking away from the real object of fear. Because of that, the popular culture of, and particularly the televised portrayals of, natural disaster, like the flood specials, are commercially viable. Certainly other documentaries aired on TV might explore more of the historical, human element in natural disaster. Yet these are rare and still rely on production techniques that make TV interesting to look at.

Television is not as ideal an archivist as it is a creator of aesthetically pleasing, exciting visual dramas. One cannot help but reach such a conclusion, especially considering what has been left out of all of the TV renditions and commemorations of natural disaster discussed here—the human role in continued destruction of built environments. Other accounts of midwest flood history, for example, have delved more deeply into the history of major rivers and human intervention on them. The federal government-commissioned Galloway Report (Platt, 1999) is a close examination of past and present levee construction in Missouri and Illinois. In 1996, Scott Faber, of the organization called American Rivers, published a document called "On Borrowed Land: Public Policies for Floodplains," which critiques intervention on the Mississippi and Missouri Rivers leading to the 1993 flood. Documents such as these, void of visuals save for a number of graphs and charts and filled with statistics and analysis, succeed in outlining the myriad reasons rivers flood. Television offers something else.

It seems necessary to return to the idea that in all of these televised renditions of natural disaster, the medium is doing what it does best. Accurate, critical, historical, and in-depth analysis is not that. Television offers visual drama, portraying a range of emotions and the complexity of audiovisual stimulation. Although it can be quite pleasing aesthetically, there are consequences, perhaps quite sobering, to consider. Television creates an environment where dramatic visual spectacle is the norm, the expected. The outstanding visual capability overshadows language. Language, taking a back seat, becomes, as Stephens (1998) explained, something completely different in the visual medium. Visuals set the pace, create the tone, and draw us into a whole sensory environment—a place without history, without a future, and without material consequences.

6

Understanding Place, TV News, and Natural Disaster

Although the Great Flood of 1993 on the Mississippi River and the 1997 flood on the Red River really did happen, the medium of TV uniquely reshaped and re-presented them—in effect reconstructed them as major natural disaster events in the heartland. Reconstructing these events for the screen was actually a twofold process. First, network and local news organizations chose to broadcast reports on the flood for a certain time period. Drawing from broad cultural understanding about the midwest, flooding rivers and cultural discourses about nature, and formulas and routines of TV reporting, news personnel made choices about how and how long the storyline would develop and what images and references would be most appropriate for each flood story. Second, TV's aesthetic vision, its production techniques, and the broadcast infrastructure as a whole molded the flood images, references, and narratives into something uniquely televisual. Television created for us an understanding of these natural disasters that resonated with, yet transformed, the nation's understandings about nature and the midwest and in a way no other medium could.

Attempting to understand the phenomenon of natural disaster as a cultural construction and as a TV event, as the preceding chapters have, requires that we turn again to a broad theoretical framework that helps us think about the processes of communication and culture in shaping, even constructing, the world as we know it. It is especially important to include in that framework an understanding of the significance of communication technologies in reality construction. Media Ecology provides the appropriate framework. The works of Carey (1988) and Meyrowitz (1995, 1998) are especially pertinent to this broadest of theoretical umbrellas. Both scholars recognized and emphasized the significance of the communication medium in shaping and understanding the social world and relationships in that world. Carey's and Meyrowitz's Media Ecology frameworks fit well into the broader category of academic practice called *cultural studies*, particularly the North American variety, as Flayhan (2001) argued. North American cultural studies, with roots in the intellectual work of Dewey, Goffman, and Park, among others, is interdisciplinary and places great emphasis on communication and culture. Communication is viewed as a process of meaning making, and the form of communication, not just the content, is seen as a significant factor in that meaning-making process (Flayhan, 2001).

Carey's ritual view of communication—especially his focus on the significance of changes in dominant media—and Meyrowitz's medium theory are both elegant and clear models for understanding, in broadest terms, how we come to know and understand our environment as a whole. In this particular study, the focus is our understanding of and relationship to nature, how we understand and define natural disaster, and how these understandings are necessarily related to place meaning and understanding. The ritual view of communication emphasizes communication as a process through which the world is made to mean (Carey, 1988). Changes in communication media significantly alter the meaning-making process, and thus the understanding, of various aspects of the social world. Medium theory focuses on how different media, because of inherent biases, allow different patterns of access to information and differently shape perceptions (Meyrowitz, 1985). Both Carey and Meyrowitz focus on electronic media and the cultural changes that coincide with the onset of electronic communication as the dominant form.

This study draws from a variety of disciplines, including cultural geography, history, critical media studies, and media aesthetics, especially the work of Zettl, to present an argument for the unique televisual constructions and meanings of natural disaster in one place. Therefore it fits within the parameters of media ecology and cultural studies work.

Much of the focus here is on the techniques and characteristics of the medium of TV. Media ecology's emphasis on the revolution of images in electronic media helps us understand and appreciate the power and significance of not only the specific image choices, juxtapositions, and alterations on the screen, but also the fact that TV brings the event to us in visual as opposed to print form. Besides TV form, TV content is also examined here. The study looks at TV content in terms of the use of predominant images and themes that recall cultural myths and ideologies of nature, region, and national identity. Television news about the midwest floods—both form and content—has shaped our collective understanding and memory of how these natural phenomena ought to be regarded, and how nature should behave in one region of the United States.

What we learn by examining TV news flood coverage can be broadened to a discussion of TV, natural disaster, and place more generally. What follows are the main points about TV coverage of the floods and how the medium has shaped our understanding of them, as developed in the preceding chapters. The discussion moves then beyond the floods to the broader implications of natural disasters and TV. This discussion includes a look at the sociocultural contexts of natural disasters as related to communication technologies, the implications and recommendations for understanding natural disaster news coverage from other places, and the implications and recommendations for understanding environmental practice, policy, and rhetoric in an electronic media environment. Finally, the book concludes with a few words about communication technology generally and the subsequent impact on our social and environmental behavior.

THE MIDWEST FLOODS

An interdisciplinary approach to culture and communication helps us understand that nature and place are both social constructions. Although there is an objective reality to organic and mineral beings, our understanding of and communications about them take place through our relationships with them, which we establish chiefly through our cultural filtering mechanisms, including systems of representation, belief systems, and communication tools. Television, a unique electronic communication tool, constructed the midwest floods of 1993 and 1997, visually presenting them as battles with Mother Nature in the mythic heartland.

The heartland is a geographic and ideological site. Its image and our understanding of it is part of a longer historic tradition in Western thought generally and in this country in particular. Part of how we understand the heartland is through the verbal and visual images and representations available in a variety of media forms, including books, paintings and other art works, film, radio, and TV. Heartland imagery generally calls up notions of a bucolic pastoral landscape—nature in submission to the agrarian ideal. Such imagery has persisted for decades and beyond and was dredged up once again in local and network TV news coverage of the 1993 and 1997 midwest floods.

News is a socioculturally sanctioned form of telling and, through a unique format, constructs its own reality. Television news has a particular way of telling and constructing. Its spatial and expressive biases render it a means for intimate yet emotionally jarring visual images of nature, disaster, and human suffering. Television gives us visual and aural access to information, events, and phenomena in a way that print media cannot. During coverage of the 1993 and 1997 floods, TV called up familiar heartland imagery, but imprinted it with TV's own electronic logic. Television as an electronic communication mechanism has a unique production aesthetic, a unique distribution infrastructure, and an economic imperative. None of these can be separated out when considering the significance, quality, and meaning of flood coverage.

Television techniques and TV news format drew from and extended the mythic agrarian heartland in continuous disaster reporting on the small screen. Specific types of editing, camera use, computer graphics, and the overall presentation and organization of the newscasts worked together to create and reinforce the idea of a battle between humans and nature. Nature was pitted as the enemy against human (particularly midwestern) victims who were constructed as a collective protagonist fighting in solidarity against the waters' onslaught. Various images (e.g., the lines of sandbaggers and the American flag) were used over and over in TV flood stories to reinforce the theme of solidarity and unity.

The geography of flood news—that is, the source from which it was generated—made a difference in terms of overall emphasis. Network news differed from local television news in the extent to which the news teams were socially and economically tied to the area, and to the extent each had something at stake beyond the ability to gather news. Local news reported more on the political and economic implications of the flooding than did network news, which focused more on the heartland gone wrong idea. Overall, TV news generally was much more focused on visually displaying a violation of the appropriate cultural construction of nature in the midwest and the victimization of residents against the onslaught of nature than on looking long and hard at the history of human intervention on the rivers.

Besides the selective focus of TV news, there are other implications to the way in which local and network news teams covered the floods; these fall within the realm of ethics. Ethical considerations become apparent when considering the technological, geographical, aesthetic, and commercial constraints placed on TV news. However, the extent to which ethical arguments and issues can be raised regarding TV news flood coverage is determined by, and must be understood in relation to, the biases of the TV medium, or what Zettl (1990) referred to as TV doing what it does best. What TV does best is offer an appealing series of moving pictures and exciting graphics. It is highly limited as a source of complex information; therefore, as a source of news, it must be judged accordingly.

Flood coverage was an instance (in both cases) where TV could flex its aesthetic muscles, particularly in its popular flood commemorations. Commemorative videotapes, locally and nationally produced, emphasized war with nature and community solidarity. They showcased not only the heroism of those fighting nature, but also the heroism exhibited by news stations. The tapes have visually imprinted the floods in the nation's collective memory and continually serve as the popular flood archives. Considering the strengths and weaknesses, the constraints and the biases, of TV, the implications of TV serving as popular archive of these two historical events are significant and quite sobering. Residing in the popular collective memory are the most sensational, awesome, and horrific images of disaster wrought by nature on a rampage.

Yet TV's flood depictions shaped the entire range of popular culture items, artifacts, and practices that erupted from the floods. The battle and solidarity themes present in TV news were also present in a whole array of flood culture, including exhibits, books, performances, and commodity items available in various midwest locales hit hard by either flood. Together with and because of TV, flood culture has become flood folklore. The popular culture encapsulates our collective anxieties not only about nature but about ourselves in relation to nature.

Midwest flood depictions on TV are much like other televised natural disaster depictions. Videotaped renditions of disaster—be they documentary or completely fictional portrayals—have become more popular and widely available with the increase in outlets for video production and distribution. Television's unique aesthetic, its means of shaping our understanding of nature, and its need to feed the visually consuming beast that is the collective of audience members hungry for more nature drama—and in need of an enemy outside itself—churns out more and more natural disaster videos. Yet they tend to look and sound alike. The reason for this has to do with the medium, but also with the sociocultural context that is a part of our electronic media environment.

THE CONTEXT OF NATURAL DISASTER TV IN AN
ELECTRONIC MEDIA ENVIRONMENT

What are the implications of TV portrayals of natural disaster, whether fictional or nonfiction, beyond the 1993 and 1997 midwest floods? What can we learn about nature and place, and the significance of TV, from studying TV flood coverage? Perhaps we first need to look more closely at the sociocultural contexts of natural disaster coverage to help us understand how we have come to our present shared understandings about nature and place. What is it about this time in history, our geographic position in the United States, and our dominant media environment that begets the televised natural disaster coverage we have seen and are likely to see more and more? Looking beyond the floods to natural disasters more generally requires that we situate ourselves in time, place, and technological milieu.

We are living in a time of increased environmental awareness, and the public discourses of environmentalism, environmental policy, and environmental action have escalated as more and more voices, more and more interests, become involved. Environmental groups, politicians, ordinary citizens, and, of course, corporations recognize the significance of the natural environment—as a resource, a sacred entity, an issue for power-brokering and manipulation, and even a commodity. Today being green can mean many different things. It can mean you harbor concerns about preserving the environment, participate in or actively support an environmental group of some sort, pay lip service to the issue, or even have figured out how to make a lot of money from the idea of environmental awareness. Being green is, in many respects, a trendy thing to be nowadays. Who does not want to talk about environmental concerns? Unfortunately, much of it is just talk or imagery. A real understanding about what we call the *environment* requires knowledge culled from history. Historic knowledge necessarily encompasses not only the area of scientific research, but also the areas of public policy concerning nature and/or the environment, comparative nature beliefs and myths, and communications about nature—in form and content—through time. The possible breadth of understanding about nature or environment is vast and well beyond the scope of this discussion and even this study. Nevertheless, it seems clear that having a true grasp of the issue or issues requires depth of knowledge and critical awareness. Acknowledging the need to at least put things into context, here we can briefly discuss the fact that discourses about nature and the environment are clearly related to our understandings about place and to our communication technologies.

The geography of views on nature and environment—indeed the geography of nature and environment—is most telling especially when examined through time. Those who understand the unique meanings placed on different natural settings or phenomena in different parts of the United States, for example, realize the significance of place on nature. The works of Leo Marx, Simon Schama, and John Rennie Short— all of whom examine ideas about nature as a social construct in historical context—are helpful and insightful when considering the relationship between the United States and ideas and practices concerning nature. Short's (1991) book, *Imagined Country: Society, Culture and Environment* discussed the unique way in which wilderness and the country are perceived in the United States. The Romantic view of wilderness—most prevalent in the New World— is as a spiritual entity, a kind of paradise. However, the Classical view—most prevalent in Europe—was wilderness as something to be feared and overcome. Despite a predominantly Romantic view of nature and wilderness in the New World, the early Puritan settlers, Short explained, worked to tame the wilderness. Creating country or garden was a sacred act of redemption. This idea has held fast in the American imagination, in tandem with the Romantic wilderness idea. Likewise, Schama (1995), who focused on landscape, talked about wilderness as culture's craving, and how the act of visually preserving it, through art works and national parks, indicates our desire to maintain national ideals of individual freedom and openness, as opposed to the confinement represented in urban landscapes. Marx's (1964) book, *The Machine in the Garden*, explored the ideas of pastoral and wilderness in the United States, and particularly how visions of both are related to and reconciled with technology. In the United States, he argued, we hold fast to a unique kind of pastoralism— one that reflects a particularly American experience. Americans, Marx argued, idealize the pastoral and strive for a return to an Edenic state. Such a state is embodied in the idea of middle agrarian landscapes. Such landscapes (the midwest?), exist in harmony with technology. However, these ideas actually contradict the reality of urban, industrial mechanization in the nation and beyond. The idea of the pastoral, middle landscape helps us hold fast to an ordered agrarian outlook, and helps us make meaning within a reality that contradicts that outlook. These ideas about nature settings in cultural context exemplify and reinforce Anderson's (1983) idea of the nation as an imagined community. The places, spaces, and environments of nation are part of the collective imagination that comprise its sense of identity.

Meyrowitz (1985) argued that, in the age of electronic media, space does not matter anymore. His argument refers specifically to the fact that previously understood forms of social and physical space are violated or transcended because of electronic media. Although that is true, space still matters insofar as our thinking is still largely wedded to geographies as physical, ideological, and metaphorical sites. Technology necessarily changes how we think of space and place, yet we tend to hold fast to old ideas in the midst of new—a point Marx made in his work. Morley and Robins (1995) explained that new electronic media are constructing new geographies, in effect reordering our experience and creating a new sense of place as opposed to no sense of place. The new sense of place changes how we experience place for ourselves and others in other places and other environments. Marx submitted that we are merely fooling ourselves by trying to ignore the contradictions between ideal environments and technological realities, but perhaps it is more accurate to say we are struggling with the dialectic. The force behind it is the shift in dominant communication forms; the site is the collection of places or environments we imagine as well as live in. We return to the idea that a shift from print- to electronic-based media signals a shift in thinking and representing. Much of TV content represents continuity with print, whereas the electronic form is radically different, representing change. Regarding TV and depictions of nature or natural environments in specific places, we continue to see familiar visual imagery and themes—those that reinforce older ideas about what those places and environments mean. Yet TV offers them in a vastly different form. They are almost strictly visual and significantly televisual. That is, they are edited, altered, and formatted uniquely for the TV screen. The result is a changed way of seeing them and thinking about them and about ourselves in relation to them. The tension between the old and new is not insignificant. After all, the way we understand those places and the nature in them explains who we are.

Television's representations of nature and place help us understand them and the kind of relationship we have or should have with them. For example, nightly televised midwest flood coverage consisted mostly in a few minutes' worth of images and sounds edited in tight, quickly paced packages. As more thoroughly explained in chapter 4, the content of the images—the agrarian icons representing a vast array of pastoral values—appeared in a format that encouraged emotional involvement with a drama pitting human victims against a raging natural force. In this instance, the entire aesthetic of TV encouraged us to experience—in a speeded up, emotionally charged and aesthetically rich way—the violation of the heartland myth. Through TV, we were recognizing and reconnecting with our national identity vis-à-vis the heartland and all it stands for. Yet the way in which we reconnected was compressed, fragmented, immediate, and out of context. The broader implications of the disaster, including the history of the use of technology and of the lands and rivers, were virtually left out. We were encouraged to visualize and relate to the immediate human suffering and the plight of those who happened to be caught unaware of what was reported to be a freak natural occurrence. We were not encouraged to consider the politics behind the floods, the broader and deeper reasons that floods occurred in the past, why they occurred in 1993 and 1997, and why, no doubt, they will continue to occur.

Interestingly, TV flood coverage was a contradictory display of the Romantic and Classical views of nature. Prominent throughout coverage of both floods was the idea that the rivers should be tamed and controlled lest they wreak more havoc on those who have also chosen to tame the lands surrounding the water. The Army Corps of Engineers and other flood control experts were portrayed in the capacity to employ correct technology in that effort. Unbeknownst to TV news personnel, the technology of TV was perhaps the largest, most concentrated effort at flood control. Yet at times during the course of flood reporting, news personnel indicated an underlying awe of and respect for the power of the water. A tinge of Romanticism crept into coverage now and again. The most obvious places were in those news stories where Dan Rather, Peter Jennings, Tom Brokaw, or even one of the network correspondents waxed nostalgic about Old Man River, quoted Mark Twain, or used another literary or folkloric reference to the awesome power of nature and the comparative futility of human efforts. Contradictions like this are perfectly acceptable on TV. Juxtaposing two opposing views of nature in relationship to culture works from an aesthetic point of view, if not a critical one. The relationship with the rivers that we were encouraged to retain was still one of awe and fear, and with the heartland one of yearning.

Television draws its own maps that extend beyond the screen to our collective identifications with place and nature. Television creates places and events that exist nowhere but on the screen, but our relationships to those places and the environment in general, although virtual, are intimate and emotional. Television is the ideal forum for displaying disaster—hence, our current proliferation of doomsday imagery on the tube. The production techniques are awesome, and the disasters created on TV ask us to recall our collective responses to natural forces. Because of TV's emphasis on the now and its audiovisual sensory stimulation, we can easily project our fears about the future and our role in constructing that future onto nature. Natural disaster TV is enticing because it obscures the political and economic factors, our own efforts, that contribute to these Acts of God and/or nature. We construct our own enemy and make sure it is not us.

In depicting natural disaster, TV becomes both a source and a response. Natural disaster displays on TV are responsive ritual events. We participate in a reassertion of our rights, dominance, solidarity, and identity. Natural disaster displays help us understand and celebrate who we are as a culture and as a nation. They also work as an antidote to our postindustrial, technologized, and digitized existence. Television is a source of ritual, but it also creates ritual. News functions to capture and canonize certain historic events and moments as Zelizer (1993a) argued. Journalists and news organizations become cultural authorities, authorized to shape, interpret, and present certain events and phenomena. Television journalists specifically are given such authority because the medium constructs the parameters of authority. Electronic communication sets the parameters of expectation and stimulation. Its expressive bias directs us to become engrossed in its worldview and adhere to its rules of discussion and representation. That includes directing us to the authorized tellers. Television is, in McLuhan's phrasing, an extension of our nervous system, but it is also an extension of our entire system of cultural authority.

NATURAL DISASTER NEWS IN OTHER PLACES

Insofar as TV is a vital medium in the shaping of new geographies, and in light of the focus here on televised disaster portrayals within the United States, we must move out and consider disaster portrayals in other nations, and other places. Even as we define ourselves, Americans, in terms of the places and nature within our own nation, so too do we understand ourselves in comparison with our understanding of those in other places and environments. As Coker (1992) explained, "Everything on the screen says something about ourselves. It challenges us to respond, to relate what we see to what we are. It compels us to validate our own identity" (p. 197).

Much has been written about the quantity and some about the quality of news from the U.S. press about places outside the United States, and most notably the Developing World. Most of the scholarly research on international disaster coverage in the U.S. press consists in quantitative content analyses of the sheer amount of coverage about certain disasters in certain regions of the world. Typically these studies compare coverage of disasters in the First World with Disasters in the Third World. Whether analyzing print and broadcast news, or just broadcast coverage on the three major networks, most of the studies to date have found that, indeed, the U.S. press is biased in its disaster reporting. That is, the time and space devoted to reports of specific disasters from around the world in U.S. newspapers and on U.S.-based TV networks indicates that the United States prioritizes the rest of the world and gives higher priority to First World disasters than to Third World disasters. Following is a look at a very small sample of many like studies published within the past 20+ years. Adams (1986), who examined the amount of time ABC, CBS, and NBC news gave to a range of highly consequential (in terms of lives lost) disasters that occurred from 1972 to 1985, found that a country's cultural proximity to the United States, its distance from New York City, and the estimated number of deaths all accounted for disparity in TV disaster coverage from around the world. He concluded that major disasters in what he called the Third World receive proportionately little attention. Gaddy and Tanjong (1986), who looked at U.S. newspaper and TV coverage of 1982 and 1983 earthquakes, found that 71% of them were reported from developing nations. Focusing on the number of reports, the total story length, and the priority given the story, Gaddy and Tanjong concluded that the quantity of coverage of a disaster story was not determined by the geography, but by the human and physical consequences of the disaster, including number dead or injured and degree of physical damage. Finally, Singer, Endreny and Glassman (1991) examined U.S. media disaster coverage. They found that geography does matter. In summary, they examined how different types of disasters, including natural and technological disasters, were covered in various media outlets, and found that news about natural disasters in the United States is given disproportionate attention in the U.S. press. In other words, by giving these stories more space and time than disaster stories from other nations, there is a bias toward covering disasters that occur in the United States.

Although the three studies mentioned earlier specifically emphasize the geographic significance of disaster coverage in the media, by focusing only on numbers— specifically the amount and priority of coverage—and by not directly addressing the vast differences between newspaper and TV coverage generally, they miss much of the significance of comparative disaster news, particularly in terms of its geographic significance. Consequently, the studies give us little information about quality of disaster news, including what news coverage of disasters in other places tell us about our understanding of the environments and people in those places, what that says about us, and what that says about the communication media we attend to and rely on for learning about and sharing information about other places and people. Two of the three studies (Adams, 1986; Gaddy & Tanjong, 1986) looked exclusively at natural disaster news, and only one examined TV coverage only (Adams, 1986). By not discussing the differences in types of disaster—although this was not the intent of the authors—and by not distinguishing TV from newspaper coverage, Singer, Endreny, and Glassman (1991) did not and cannot give us much significant information about news coverage from other places in the U.S. media. Knowing only that geography of the story makes a difference does not get us far, and merely skims the surface of possibilities for knowing and understanding the reasons for such difference. Neither does it really tell us about the geographies of difference created through different media and how that translates into understanding beyond geography.

It would be much more interesting and telling in a deeper cultural sense if studies such as these, in looking at international natural disaster coverage exclusively, explored how and why various media construct the places and people they do. As argued before, focusing on these areas would lead to a better understanding of how we define who they are, who we are, and how the biases of communications media work to lead us to our definitions and understandings. Do the U.S. broadcast media, as Morley and Robins (1995) contended, look through *Western* eyes, continuously constructing the Other through media technologies and news outlets controlled by U.S. corporate interests? Do they, as Said (1978) argued, work against increased intercultural understanding by reinforcing existing stereotypes such as that of the demonized and mysterious Orient? Can we find instances where TV indeed offers us a glimpse of people and places representing the true cultural hybridity that is the normal state of affairs in the world (Morley & Robins, 1995)? With questions such as these in mind, we can embark on research in international natural disaster news within a more inclusive framework. Such a framework would consider technology, new geographies, and economic interests along with the specifics of the media portrayals. Following are some suggestions for the kinds of questions or areas that might be explored in future comparative natural disaster news research.

A possible line of research might include examining how the narrative of the disaster is played out in one medium over the course of coverage. If looking exclusively at TV coverage, for example, one might ask how the disaster is dramatized. What techniques of TV production construct the disaster? What themes emerge in the disaster narrative? How does TV produce those themes? More specifically, what visual, aural, and other affective elements are used to create the grand themes and sub-themes that define the disaster?

Moving on from there, one might examine the kinds of relationships represented in the news coverage. What is the relationship of people to the land in these televised portrayals of natural disaster? What assumptions are made about the land and environment in that place? How does TV construct and express a relationship between culture and nature?

Finally, but not exhaustively, a number of other factors might be considered. What is the source of news? Is it a broadcast network with tight time constraints? Is it a cable network where more and longer coverage is possible? What is the national origin of the news source? What has been the history between the nation reporting and the nation reported on? What has been the history between the news source and the nation reported on? How might these factors affect the quality of coverage?

Although these questions are only a beginning, they offer a way to move beyond looking at one natural disaster in one nation to other natural disasters in other nations, with the aim of reaching a greater understanding of ourselves and our environments in the increasingly important and larger context of the interdependence of people, places, and natural environments in a world dominated, and in many ways created, by electronic media.

FINAL THOUGHTS ON THE FRAMEWORK FOR UNDERSTANDING NATURE, PLACE, AND TV

Media ecology, within a larger cultural studies framework, opens up new ways to understand how communication media shape how we understand nature and place, and how nature and place, as sociocultural concepts, are directly related to technologies of communication. Within that understanding, we can explore how electronic communications media have an impact on our understanding of nature and environment, on environmental rhetoric, and on subsequent environmental and land-use policies. We can also move in a new direction while assessing the geographies of electronic media, specifically in terms of research and discussion about the ways in which other people and other places are constructed vis-à-vis televised international natural disaster news.

Obviously the areas outlined earlier hinge on assessing and understanding electronic communications, our newest and increasingly most dominant media forms. Although this book has focused almost exclusively on TV, still a prominent form of communication worldwide, one must consider it in the context of other electronic media—most notably computer-mediated forms of communication such as the Internet. The Internet is an emerging and fascinating digital hybrid of visual, verbal, and textual communication offering communication contexts that can be at once interpersonal, community-based, cross-cultural, and even international. All of those terms change, of course, in the world of Internet communication—therefore, in this digital realm, the idea of new geographies becomes something altogether different, beyond TV.

The arguments presented in this study regarding nature, place, and television might not apply to nature, place and the Internet. Only a thorough assessment of the direction, infrastructure, and aesthetics of that medium can determine for sure. This book calls for such a research endeavor.

Another call, perhaps a caution, is to avoid falling into dichotomous traps of thinking with regard to technology and nature. One trap to steer clear of is the trap of the technological sublime, as Flayhan (2001) suggested, when assessing how electronic communication impact nature and place and how we understand and react to them. To do so would be to either completely vilify new electronic media or enthusiastically celebrate its positive potential. It would be easy to make clear-cut value judgments about how TV or other electronic media change, for better or worse, our relationships with the natural environment. Indeed a case can be made for either. It is perhaps more useful to acknowledge that TV, for one, certainly *has* created change. The quality and consequence of that change must first be understood. If one is not pleased with the change one might use one's understanding of the medium's logic and its characteristics to work toward another kind of understanding and action where nature and/or place are concerned. DeLuca (1999) described how Greenpeace and other grassroots environmental justice groups have done just that. By creating image events or engaging in what he called *tactics*, for the TV screen specifically, environmental justice groups turn complex environmental issues into symbols, often in shocking or at least unorthodox ways. When people pay attention to these staged events, the thinking goes, they take notice of the issue and are more prone to seek out more information, or at the very least become aware of the situation. As Greenpeace has effectively demonstrated, an understanding of the medium must come first because the medium has set the parameters of discussion.

A second trap to avoid is persistent thinking about nature in either the Romantic or Classical views: nature as spiritual Eden or nature as conquerable resource—there for our taking. We have constructed nature in these terms, and it is from these opposing points of view that most rhetoric and debate concerning nature and environment is constructed. DeLuca (1999) explained that radical environmental justice groups have moved beyond the dichotomy. These groups, he argued, constantly deconstruct the modern ideograph of nature as a realm separate from humanity, and view the environment more holistically, as the context of people and the places where they live, play, and work. Nature or the environment is not just the remote and pristine wilderness areas separated from our daily routines. The environment includes people and encompasses issues that include socioeconomic justice.

Steinberg (2000) concurred. In the discourses of natural disaster, most often we see nature as the problem, he pointed out. Yet the problem is more accurately one of human inequity and lack of justice, which translates into lack of environmental justice and often leads to disasters for humans that involve the natural environment.

Therefore, it seems the process of thinking about nature in different terms is necessarily tied to thinking about people, relationships in general, and the processes of life in different terms. Media ecology reminds us, rather instructs us, that communications media inform our thinking about and relationships with people, places, and nature. Therefore, the technologies of communication must be a part of this change process. How much hope do we have for a new politics of the environment if we must rely on television or other electronic media forms to communicate and engage us in environmental discourse? Anderson (1997) demonstrated in her work that environmental reporting is heavily influenced by cultural values. There is an underlying moral structure to such reporting, she argued, and certain issues receive news attention because they resonate with certain cultural values and fears. De Luca (1999) suggested that the radical tactics engaged in by environmental justice groups are necessarily tempered by the likes of the big networks and their ilk who are most concerned with the status quo and, more specifically, the bottom line. He asks, "If NBC is televising the resistance, how radical can it be?" (p. 83). Postman (1985) strongly argued that TV is most capable as an entertainment medium alone.

Despite TV's limitations as a social/environmental justice medium, we must still consider its potential as we continually make ourselves aware of its power. After all, some battles have already been won via televised tactics, as DeLuca made clear. Television has the aesthetic power, but it is not in the right hands. It is quite possible that in time the conflict simmering between those who persist in old ways of thinking about nature and environment—and who work hard to retain the modern view of nature—and those who embrace the postmodern, holistic view of environment as social will erupt in a grand rhetorical and technological showdown. Perhaps electronic communication, maybe TV, will be the forum and perhaps the impetus for environmental politics, despite the current climate of monolithic media conglomeration. The potential for this happening becomes greater as natural disasters continue to appear on the TV screen at their current frequency and pace. We may yet make use of TV's aesthetic, social, and technological power to reinvent nature and place.

References

Adams, W.C. (1986). Whose lives count? TV coverage of natural disasters. *Journal of Communication, 36,* 113–122.

Alford, R.R. (1998). *The craft of inquiry: Theories, methods, evidence.* New York: Oxford University Press.

Altheide, D. (1976). *Creating reality: How TV news distorts events.* Beverly Hills: Sage.

Anderson, A. (1997). *Media, culture and environment.* New Brunswick, NJ: Rutgers University Press.

Anderson, B. (1983). *Imagined communities: Reflections on the origin and spread of nationalism.* London: Verso.

Anderson, G.C., & Woolworth A.R. (Eds.). (1988). *Through Dakota eyes: Narrative accounts of the Minnesota Indian war of 1862.* St. Paul: Minnesota Historical Society Press.

Anderson, M.G., & Platt, R.H. (1999). St. Charles county, Missouri: Federal dollars and the 1993 midwest flood. In R.H. Platt (Ed.), *Disasters and democracy: The politics of extreme natural events* (pp. 215–239). Washington, DC: Island Press.

Averille, T.F. (1999). Flyover country: An introduction. *The North American Review, 284,* 4.

Barcott, B. (2001, July/August). For God so loved the world: Evangelicals and other faithful preach the green gospel. *Utne Reader, 106,* 50–56.

Barry, J.M. (1997). *Rising tide: The great Mississippi flood of 1927 and how it changed America.* New York: Simon & Schuster.

Barthes, R. (1972). *Mythologies* (Annette Lavers, Trans.). New York: Hill & Wang.

Beebe, T.O. (1995). Talking maps: Regions and revolution in Juan Vincent Benet and Euclides de Cunha. *Comparative Literature, 47,* 193.

Benjamin, W. (1968). The work of art in the age of mechanical reproduction. In H. Arendt (Ed.), *Illuminations* (pp. 217–252). New York: Schocken.

Bird, E. (1996). CJ's revenge: Media, folklore, and the cultural construction of AIDs. *Critical Studies in Mass Communication, 13,* 44-58.

Bird, S.E., & Dardenne, R.W. (1988). Myth, chronicle and story: Exploring the narrative qualities of news. In J. Carey (Ed.), *Media, myths and narratives: Television and the press* (pp. 67-86). Newbury Park: Sage.

Bloom, H. (Ed.). (1987). *Willa Cather's My Antonia.* New York: Chelsea House.

Boorstin, D.J. (1972). *The image: A guide to pseudo-events in America.* New York: Atheneum.

Bradshaw, M. (1988). *Regions and regionalism in the U.S.* Houdsmills, England: Macmillan.

Browne, W.P., Skees, J.R., Swanson, L.E., Thompson, P.B., & Unnevehr, L.J. (1992). *Sacred cows and hot potatoes: Agrarian myths in agricultural policy.* Boulder, CO: Westview.

Burch, W.R., Jr. (1984). Nature and society—seeking the ghost in the sociological machine. *Communication Quarterly, 32,* 9-19.

Burgess, J., & Gold, J.R. (1985). *Geography, media and popular culture.* London: Croom Helm.

Burgess, J. (1990). Landscape representations in the media. *Landscape Research, 15,* 7–11.

Carey, J. (1988). *Communication as culture: Essays on media and society.* Boston: Unwin Hyman.

Carstensen, V. (1965). The development and application of regional concepts, 1900-1950. In M. Jensen (Ed.), *Regionalism in America* (pp. 99–118). Westport, CT: Greenwood.

Carter, T.M. (1980). Community warning systems: The relationships among the broadcast media, emergency service agencies, and the National Weather Service. In *Disasters and the Mass Media: Proceedings of the Committee on Disasters and the Mass Media Workshop 1979.* Committee on Disasters and the Mass Media (pp. 214–228). Washington, DC: National Academy of Sciences.

Cartwill, M. (1993). *A view to a death in the morning: Hunting and nature through history.* Cambridge, MA: Harvard University Press.

Cather, W. (1918). *My Antonia*. New York: Houghton Mifflin.

Charlier, T. (2000. June 12). Plan would reconnect lower Mississippi with its flood plain and back channels. Scripps Howard News Service. *Pittsburgh Post-Gazette*, p. A8.

Christensen, L., & Ruch, C.E. (1978). Assessment of brochures and radio and television presentations on hurricane awareness. *Mass Emergencies, 3,* 209–216.

Cohen, A. (1998). Between content and cognition: On the impossibility of television news. *Communications: The European Journal of Communication Research, 23,* 447–461.

Coker, C. (1992). Post-modernity and the end of the cold war: Has war been dis-invented? *Review of International Studies, 18,* 189–198.

Cosgrove, D., & Daniels, S. (1988). *The iconography of landscapes.* Cambridge: Cambridge University Press.

Crawford, A. (1992). Landscape photography as art. *Landscape Research, 17,* 2–9.

Daniels, S. (1991). The making of Constable Country 1880-1940. *Landscape Research, 16,* 9–17.

Daniels, S., & Cosgrove, D. (1993). Spectacle and text: Landscape metaphors in cultural geography. In J. Duncan & D. Ley (Eds.), *Place/culture/representation* (pp. 57–77). London: Routledge.

Davidson, O.G. (1990). *Broken heartland: The rise of America's rural ghetto.* New York: The Free Press.

de Certeau, M. (1984). *The practice of everyday life.* Berkeley: University of California Press.

Dietrich, W. (1995). *The great Columbia River.* New York: Simon & Schuster.

DeLuca, K. (1996). Constructing nature anew through judgment: The possibilities of media. In S. Muir & T.L. Veenendall (Eds.), *Earthtalk: Communication and empowerment for environmental action* (pp. 59–78). Westport, CT: Praeger.

DeLuca, K. (1999). *Image politics: The new rhetoric of environmental activism.* New York: Guilford.

Dennis, J.M. (1998). *Renegade regionalists: The modern independence of Grant Wood, Thomas Hart Benton, and John Steuart Curry.* Madison: The University of Wisconsin Press.

Deppa, J. (1994). *The media and disaster: Pan Am 103.* New York: New York University Press.

Dirks, N.B., Eley, G., & Ortner, S.B. (Eds.). (1994). *Culture/power/history: A reader in contemporary social theory.* Princeton, NJ: Princeton University Press.

Dorson, R.M. (Ed.). (1983). *Handbook of American folklore.* Bloomington: Indiana University Press.

Dudley, K.M. (2000). *Debt and dispossession: Farm loss and America's heartland.* Chicago: The University of Chicago Press.

Duncan, J., & Ley, D. (1993). *Place/culture/representation.* London: Routledge.

Douglas, M. (1966). *Purity and danger: An analysis of concepts of pollution and taboo*. New York: Praeger.

Egan, T. (2001, June 3). As whites leave great plains, Indians, buffalo are returning. *Minneapolis Star Tribune*, p. A15.

Elliot, D. (1989). Tales from the dark side: Ethical implications of disaster coverage. In L.M. Walters, L. Wilkins, & T. Walters (Eds.), *Bad tidings: Communication and catastrophe* (pp. 161–170). Hillsdale, NJ: Lawrence Erlbaum.

Epstein, E.J. (1973). *News from nowhere: Television and the news*. New York: Vintage Books.

Faber, S. (1996). *On borrowed land: Public policies for floodplains*. Cambridge, MA: Lincoln Institute of Land Policy.

Fiske, J. (1989). *Reading the popular*. Boston: Unwin Hyman.

Flayhan, D.P. (2001). Cultural studies and media ecology: Meyrowitz's medium theory and Carey's cultural studies. *The New Jersey Journal of Communication, 9*, 21–44.

Foss, S. (1989). *Rhetorical criticism: Exploration and practice*. Prospect Heights, IL: Waveland.

Foucault, M. (1980). Questions of geography. In C. Gordon (Ed.), *Power/knowledge: Selected interviews and other writings, 1972–1977* (pp. 146–165). New York: Pantheon.

Fry, K. (1994). *Old south, agrarian midwest and frontier west: Discourses of repression and consumption in regional consumer magazines*. Unpublished doctoral dissertation, Temple University, Philadelphia, PA.

Fry, K. (1995). Regional consumer magazines and the ideal white reader: Constructing and retaining geography as text. In D. Abrahamson (Ed.), *The American magazines: Research perspectives and prospects* (pp. 186–204). Ames: Iowa State University Press.

Fry, K. (1998). A cultural geography of Lake Wobegon. *Howard Journal of Communication, 4*, 303–321.

Fuller, P. (1985). *Images of God: The consolidation of lost illusions*. London: Writers and Readers Publishing Cooperative.

Gaddy, G.D., & Tanjong, E. (1986). Earthquake coverage by the western press. *Journal of Communication, 36*, 105–112.

Gamson, W.A. (1988). A constructionist approach to mass media and public opinion. *Symbolic Interaction, 11*, 161–174.

Gans, H.J. (1979). *Deciding what's news: A case study of CBS Evening News, NBC Nightly News, Newsweek and Time*. New York: Vintage Books.

Garner, A.C. (1992). *The disaster news story: The reader, the content and the construction of meaning*. Unpublished doctoral dissertation, University of Iowa, Iowa City, Iowa.

Garner, A.C. (1994, August). *The cost of fighting mother nature: News coverage of the 1993 midwest floods*. Paper presented at the annual meeting of the Association for Education in Journalism and Mass Communication, Atlanta, GA.

Gitlin, T. (1987). Domesticating nature. In D. Lazere (Ed.), *American media and mass culture: Left perspectives* (pp. 139–144). Berkeley: University of California Press.

Goedkoop, R.J. (1988). *Inside local television news.* Salem, WI: Sheffield.

Graber, D. (1980). *Crime news and the public.* New York: Praeger.

Graber, D. (1990). Seeing is remembering: How visuals contribute to learning from television news. *Journal of Communication, 40,* 134-155.

Griffin, M. (1992). Looking at TV news: Strategies for research. *Communication, 13,* 121–141.

Grossberg, L. (1992). *We gotta get out of this place: Popular conservatism and postmodern culture.* New York: Routledge.

Grunwald, M. (2001, May 13). Not-so-natural disasters. *Minneapolis Star Tribune,* Sunday, p. A23.

Gruffudd, P., Daniels, S., & Bishop, P. (1991). Landscape and national identity. *Landscape Research, 16,* 1–2.

Gumpert, G., & Drucker, S. (1997). *Voices in the street: Explorations in gender, media, and public space.* Cresskill, NJ: Hampton.

Haga, C. (2001, April 17). Chief tours Red, makes no promises; river town praised for their savvy in fighting floods. *Minneapolis Star Tribune,* p. 3B.

Halbwachs, M. (1992). *On collective memory* (Lewis A. Coser, Trans.). Chicago: University of Chicago Press.

Hannibal Writer's Club. (1985). *Life on the Mississippi: 100 years later.* Hannibal, MO: Author.

Haraway, D. (1989). *Primate visions: Gender, race and nature in the world of modern science.* New York: Routledge.

Harvey, D. (1989). *The condition of postmodernity: An enquiry into the origins of cultural change.* Oxford: Blackwell.

Harvey, D. (1996). *Justice, nature and the geography of difference.* Cambridge, MA: Blackwell.

Hay, J. (1993). Invisible cities/visible geographies: Toward a cultural geography of Italian TV in the 90s. *Quarterly Review of Film and Television, 14,* 35–47.

Hennen, T. (1997). *Crawling out the window.* Goodhue, MN: Black Hat Press.

Holm, B. (1985). *The music of failure.* Marshall, MN: Plains Press.

Holm, B. (1996). *The heart can be filled anywhere on earth: Minnesota, Minnesota.* Minneapolis, MN: Milkweed Editions.

Hurley, F. J. (1972). *Portrait of a decade: Roy Stryker and the development of documentary photography in the Thirties.* New York: Da Capo Press.

Hurley, J., & Hagood, R. (1993). *Hannibal Courier-Post edition of Hannibal flood '93.* Hannibal, MO: Hannibal Courier-Post.

Hylden, E., & Reuter, L. (1998). *Under the whelming tide: The 1997 flood of the Red River of the north.* Grand Forks: North Dakota Museum of Art.

Innis, H. (1951). *The bias of communication*. Toronto: The University of Toronto Press.

Jakle, J. (1987). *The visual elements of landscape*. Amherst: University of Massachusetts Press.

Jensen, M. (Ed.). (1965). *Regionalism in America*. Madison: University of Wisconsin Press.

Jonsson, P. (2001, January 26). Southern pride rising—rankling in surge of regionalism, more southerners are waving flags and defending confederate icons. *Christian Science Monitor*, p. 1.

Kelsen, H. (1946). *Society and nature — a sociological inquiry*. London: Routledge & Kegan Paul.

Keppler, H. (1996). How to photograph a landscape. *Popular Photography, 60*, 58–60.

Kinsey, J.L. (1989). *Creating a sense of place: Thomas Moran and the surveying of the American west*. Unpublished doctoral dissertation, Washington University, St. Louis, Missouri.

Kreps, G.A. (1980). Research needs and policy issues on mass media disaster reporting. In *Disasters and the Mass Media: Proceedings of the Committee on Disasters and the Mass Media Workshop 1979* (pp. 35-74). Committee on Disasters and the Mass Media. Washington, DC: National Academy of Sciences.

Kueneman, R., & Wright, J.E. (1975). News policies of broadcast stations for civil disturbances and disasters. *Journalism Quarterly, 52*, 670–677.

Larsen, S.E. (1992). Is nature really natural? *Landscape Research, 17*, 116–123.

Lasley, P., Leistritz, F.L., Lobao, L.M., & Meyer, K. (1995). *Beyond the amber waves of grain: An examination of social and economic restructuring in the heartland*. Boulder, CO: Westview.

Leeson, T. (1994). Nature's way: Is it really irrational to fear the wild? *Utne Reader, 64*, 40–41.

Lefebvre, H. (1990). *The production of space* (Donald Nicholson-Smith, trans.). Cambridge, MA: Blackwell.

Levi-Strauss, C. (1966). *The savage mind*. Chicago: University of Chicago Press.

Levine, L. (1992). The folklore of industrial society: Popular culture and its audiences. *The American Historical Review, 97*, 1396–1430.

Levy, P. (2000, November 12). The silent epidemic. *Minneapolis Star Tribune*, p. 1A.

Limerick, P.N. (1987). *The legacy of conquest: The unbroken past of the American west*. New York: Norton.

Lippert, B. (1993, June 7). Get real: NBC's week of virtual disasters showed how TV reality is collapsing into itself. *Mediaweek*, p. T24.

Malcolm, A.H., & Straus, R. III (1996). *Mississippi currents: Journeys through time and a valley*. New York: William Morrow.

Marshall, P. (1994). *Nature's web: Rethinking our place on earth*. New York: Paragon House.

Marvin, C., & Ingle, D.W. (1999). *Blood sacrifice and the nation: Totem ritu-als and the American flag*. Cambridge: Cambridge University Press.

Marx, L. (1964). *The machine in the garden: Technology and the pastoral ideal in America*. Oxford: Oxford University Press.

McCarthy, T. (2001, July 16). High noon in the west. *Time*, pp. 18–21.

McLuhan, M. (1964). *Understanding media: The extensions of man*. New York: McGraw-Hill.

McLuhan, M. (1973). At the moment of sputnik the planet became a global theater in which there are no spectators but only actors. *Journal of Communication, 24*, 48–58.

McPhee, J. (1989). *The control of nature*. New York: Farrar, Straus & Giroux.

Medsger, B. (1989, December). Earthquake shakes four newspapers. *Washington Journalism Review*, pp. 18-22

Meeds, R., & Thorson, E. (1995, May). *The framing of television stories of the midwest flood of 1993*. Paper presented at the annual meeting of the International Communication Association, Albuqurque, NM.

Meyrowitz, J. (1985). *No sense of place: The impact of electronic media on social behavior*. New York: Oxford University Press.

Meyrowitz, J. (1998). Multiple media literarcies. *Journal of Communication, 48*, 96–108.

Miller, J.E. (1987). Willa Cather's *My Antonia* and the American dream. In H. Bloom (Ed.), *Willa Cather's My Antonia* (pp. 99–108). New York: Chelsea House.

Millett, L. (2001, April 19). River swamps St. Paul again. *Saint Paul Pioneer Press*, pp. 1A, 10A.

Monmonier, M. (1989). *Maps with the news: The development of American journalistic cartography*. Chicago: The University of Chicago Press.

Morley, D., & Robins, K. (1995). *Spaces of identity: Global media, electronic landscapes and cultural boundaries*. London: Routledge.

Motz, M.F. (1981). Introduction. *Journal of Regional Cultures, 2*, 1–5.

Mukerji, C. (1984). Visual language in science and the exercise of power: The case of cartography in early modern Europe. *Studies in Visual Communication, 10*, 30-45.

Newcomb, H. (1982). Toward a television aesthetic. In H. Newcomb (Ed.), *Television: The critical view* (3rd ed., pp. 478–494). New York: Oxford University Press.

Nimmo, D., & Combs, J.E. (1985). *Nightly horrors: Crisis coverage by television network news*. Knoxville: University of Tennessee Press.

Ong, W.J. (1982). *Orality and literacy: Technologizing of the word*. London: Methuen.

Osborne, B.S. (1992). Interpreting a nation's identity: Artists as creators of national consciousness. In A.R.H. Baker & G. Biger (Eds.), *Ideology and landscape in historical perspective* (pp. 230–254). Cambridge: Cambridge University Press.

Platt, R.H. (1999). *Disasters and democracy: The politics of extreme natural events*. Washington, DC: Island Press.

Postman, N. (1985). *Amusing ourselves to death: Public discourse in the age of show business.* New York: Viking.

Postman, N., & Powers, S. (1992). *How to watch TV news.* New York: Penguin.

Powers, R. (1980). *The newscasters: The news as show business.* New York: Norton.

Pringle, T.R. (1991). Cold comfort: The popular landscape in English and American popular culture, 1845–1990. *Landscape Research, 16,* 43–48.

Purdy, J. (1999, December 20). The new culture of rural America. *The American Prospect,* pp. 26–31.

Quantic, D.D. (1997). *The nature of the place: A study of great plains fiction.* Lincoln: University of Nebraska Press.

Quarantelli, E.L. (1989). The social science study of disasters and mass communication. In L.M. Walters, L. Wilkins, & T. Walters (Eds.), *Bad tidings: Communication and catastrophe* (pp. 1–19). Hillsdale, NJ: Erlbaum.

Raphael, B. (1986). *When disaster strikes: How individuals and communities cope with catastrophe.* New York: Basic.

Reuter, L. (1998). A flood of fire and ice. In E. Hylden & L. Reuter (Eds.), *Under the whelming tide: The 1997 flood of the Red River of the north* (p. 3). Grand Forks: North Dakota Museum of Art.

Roberts, B.M., Dennis, J.M., Horns, J.S., & Parkin, H.M. (1995). *Grant Wood: An American master revealed.* San Francisco: Pomegranate Art Books.

Rogers, E.M., & Sood, R.S. (1980). Mass media communication and disasters: A content analysis of media coverage of the Andhra Pradesh cyclone and the Sahel drought. In *Disasters and the Mass Media: Proceedings of the Committee on Disasters and the Mass Media Workshop 1979* (pp. 139-157). Committee on Disasters and the Mass Media. Washington, DC: National Academy of Sciences.

Rosenblum, M. (1970). *Coups and earthquakes.* New York: Harper & Row.

Rundstrom, B. (1995). Harvesting Willa Cather's literary fields. *The Geographical Review, 85,* 217.

Saglia, D. (1996). Looking at the other: Cultural difference and the traveller's gaze in "The Italian." *Studies in the Novel, 28,* 12.

Said, E. (1978). *Orientalism.* Harmondsworth: Penguin.

Saloutos, T. (1951). *Twentieth-century populism: Agricultural discontent in the middle west, 1900-1939.* Lincoln: University of Nebraska Press.

Schama, S. (1995). *Landscape and memory.* New York: Knopf.

Schlesinger, P. (1991). *Media, state and nation: Political violence and collective identities.* London: Sage.

Seymour, S., & Watkins, C. (1995). Church, landscape and community: Rural life and the church of England. *Landscape Research, 20,* 30–44.

Shoemaker, P. (1991). *Gatekeeping.* Newbury Park, CA: Sage.

Short, J.R. (1991). *Imagined country: Society, culture and environment.* London: Routledge.

Silverstone, R. (1988). Television myth and culture. In J. W. Carey (Ed.), *Media, myths and narratives: Television and the press* (pp. 20–47). Newbury Park, CA: Sage.

Singer, E., Endreny, P., & Glassman, M.B. (1991). Media coverage of disasters: Effect of geographic location. *Journalism Quarterly, 68,* 48–58.

Slack, J.D. (1996). *Land and memory.* Paper presented at the annual meeting of the International Communication Association, Chicago.

Slotkin, R. (1992). *Gunfighter nation: The myth of the frontier in twentieth-century America.* New York: Atheneum.

Smiley, J. (1991). *A thousand acres.* New York: Fawcett Columbine.

Smith, J. (1993). The lie that blinds: Destabilizing the text of landscape. In J. Duncan & D. Ley (Eds.), *Place/culture/representation* (pp. 78–92). London: Routledge.

Smith, S.A. (1985). *Myth, media and the southern mind.* Fayetteville: The University of Arkansas Press.

Soja, E. (1989). *Postmodern geographies: The reassertion of space in critical social theory.* London: Verso.

Steinberg, T. (2000). *Acts of God: The unnatural history of natural disaster in America.* New York: Oxford University Press.

Stephens, M. (1998). *The rise of the image the fall of the word.* New York: Oxford University Press.

Storm, J. (2001, March 11). Schlock at 11: On the big three local TV stations real news is squeezed out by the silly, the superficial and the self-promoting—and fewer are watching. *Philadelphia Inquirer Magazine,* p. H01.

Torrance, J. (Ed). (1992). *The concept of nature.* New York: Oxford University Press.

Tuan, Y.-F. (1974). *Topophilia: A study of environmental perception, attitudes and values.* Englewood Cliffs, NJ: Prentice-Hall.

Tuchman, G. (1978). *Making news: A study in the construction of reality.* New York: The Free Press.

Twain, M. (1917). *Life on the Mississippi.* New York: Harper & Row.

Von Sternberg, B. (1998, August 9). The "empty middle." *Minneapolis Star Tribune,* p. 01A.

Waxman, J.J. (1973). Local broadcast gatekeeping during natural disasters. *Journalism Quarterly, 50,* 751–758.

Weber, M. (1948). *The protestant ethic and the spirit of capitalism* (Talcott Parsons, Trans.). New York: Scribner.

Wolf, R. (Ed.). (1995). *Heartland portrait: Stories and essays of rural life.* Clermont, IA: Free Rivers Press.

Worster, D. (Ed.). (1993). *Under western skies: Nature and history in the American west.* Oxford: Oxford University Press.

Zelizer, B. (1992). *Covering the body: The Kennedy assassination, the media, and the shaping of collective memory.* Chicago: The University of Chicago Press.

Zelizer, B. (1993a). Has communication explained journalism? *Journal of Communication, 43,* 80–88.

Zelizer, B. (1993b). Pioneers and plain folks: Cultural constructions of "place" in radio news. *Semiotica, 93*(3/4), 269–285.

Zelizer, B. (1998). *Remembering to forget: Holocaust memory through the camera's eye.* Chicago: The University of Chicago Press.

Zettl, H. (1981). Television aesthetics. In R.P. Adler (Ed.), *Understanding television: Essays on television as a social and cultural force* (pp. 115–141). New York: Praeger.

Zettl, H. (1990). *Sight, sound, motion: Applied media aesthetics* (2nd ed.). Belmont, CA: Wadsworth.

Zettl, H. (1998). Contextual media aesthetics as the basis for media literacy. *Journal of Communication, 48,* 81–95.

Zukin, S. (1991). *Landscapes of power: From Detroit to Disney World.* Berkeley: University of California Press.

VIDEOGRAPHY

Eifrig, E., & Furlow, G. (Producer). (1993). *The great flood of '93* [videotape]. Available from Multimedia, KSDK, Inc., St. Louis, Missouri.

Evans, M. (Editor). (1993). *Flood of 93* [videotape]. Available from KCCI-TV Broadcasting Company, Des Moines, Iowa.

Ford, F. (1998). (Writer and Director). Flood in memories [play]. Commissioned by North Dakota Museum of Art.

Garrett, J. (Producer), & Nolan, L. (Director). (1993). *The flood of '93* [videotape]. Available from the Wisconsin Collaborative Project.

Gilbert, M. (Producer). (1997). *Beyond the flood. The flood of 97: The people, their stories* [videotape]. Available from Minnesota Broadcasters Association, Minneapolis/St. Paul, Minnesota.

Grassie, J., Bruce, H. (Producer). (1997, April 22). *Red river rising.* In *Dateline NBC.* New York: NBC News.

Lafave, B. (Producer). (1994). *Back to the river.* In CBS *Prime Time Magazine.* New York: CBS News.

Lawrence, J., Dickman, S., & Sachs, L. (Producer). (1993). *Floodwatch'93: An historical perspective* [videotape]. Available from Quincy Broadcasting Company, WGEM-TV, Hannibal/Quincy, Illinois.

Lipscomb, J. (Producer). (1994). *Can't drown this town* [videotape]. In *National Geographic Explorer.* Available from National Geographic Society.

Lloyd, L.M. (Producer). (1996). *Five great weather disasters* [videotape]. Available from The Weather Channel.

Mandelberg, A. (Producer), & Nosseck, N. (Director). (1996). *Tornado* [Film]. Available from Frank & Bob Films II and Hallmark Entertainment.

McPhee, Larkin (1996). *Flood* (Larkin McPhee, Producer). In *Nova.* Boston, MA: WGBH-TV.

Resettlement Administration (Producer), & Pare Lorentz (Director). (1938). *The river* [film]. Available from National Film Archives, Washington, DC.

Setka, Al (Producer). (1993). *Floods of '93* [videotape]. Available from Palmer Communications Incorporated, WHO-TV, Des Moines, Iowa.

Snyder, Peter B. (1997). *Flood of '93*. In Hal German (Producer), CBS *Eye on People*. New York: CBS News.

Author Index

Subject Index

Lightning Source UK Ltd.
Milton Keynes UK
UKOW040145070213

205920UK00001B/3/A

9 781572 735170